Midnight Sun

By Craig Leibfreid

Day 1:

The journey home is just as much of an adventure as the rest of the trip, but the only good way to tell a story is to start at the beginning. When I landed at the airport in Oslo, Norway Saturday June 18th, I had been awake for the past 24 hours. It was 9:00 AM Norway time. As I waited for my bag to make its way onto the carousel, the slight anxiety from fear of lost baggage kept me awake. The lack of sleep started to send my perception askew. My brain screamed for sleep, and my eyes and ears were beginning to pay the price. From what I could see before me I was in Norway. The airport was linear with lots of wood and glass. This modern Scandinavian construct spoke to me in quiet, ever-flowing tones, tones that blew across the tongue and rolled over the lips. The interior of the building was soft and quiet. It looked like a mountain cabin turned into an airport. Nothing obsessively commercialized. My Mountainsmith backpack found its way back to me and the anxiety quieted for the moment, but the adrenaline continued to flow. I weighed the possibility of catching some sleep when I arrived at the apartment where I would spend the night. "Sleep!" I thought, "just a quick nap." With my pack securely strapped around my shoulders, I navigated the airport towards the train station. It wasn't a far walk. Out the gates, a tenth of a mile down the breezeway, and I was at computer-automated-ticketing. I was instructed to take the train to Kongsberg (Oslo Sentrum), the section of Oslo I would meet Einar. I made my way to the kiosk where I could buy my train ticket, I found I Kongsberg on the list and tried to finalize the transaction. When I tried to pay I forgot how long it takes the embedded chip in a credit card to be read and complete the transaction. I pulled my card out too quickly, and the screen said 'Transaction Canceled'. I felt panic set in. I had not been in-country for a full hour yet, and I was already stranded, or so I thought. It was my first lick of culture shock. I felt stranded. I took a few deep breaths and reasoned with the situation, and I quickly remembered the chip in the card.

After the next attempt I had my train ticket and passed through the transom that coupled the train platform to the airport. I stood on the #4 platform and waited for ten minutes. The way the light broke through the window felt like a dawning to the world. Brilliance would not be the word I'd use. It was more like the best cup of coffee on a groggy morning. No noise. A number of people, but little activity. The platform was vast, yet sheltered with a high roof and tall glass walls. There was nothing to be seen on the other side, but there was an airy spaciousness that harmonized with the vacuum within my skull. The ride was all that mattered. Important, significant moments arrived at finite time for the individual, but importance was riding its continuous rails, impacting life in a constant manner across space. 10:03 was my significant moment. The southbound train arrived, orange, and blue, and dynamic. I entered, tossed my bag on the rack overhead, and sat down. The train started moving and accelerated forward with great force. It pushed me back in my seat. I was impressed, and I wondered how far was Kongsberg if it took twenty minutes to arrive at such a high rate of speed. There were half a dozen stops along the way. Otherwise, it was smooth with uninterrupted momentum. We glided along the rails at what felt like 90 miles per hour. The inside of the railcar was comforting with its cleanliness. Hard plastic, light and dark grey. The landscape on the other side of the window began rural as we departed from the airport. Slowly, houses sat in closer proximity to each other. Then buildings became larger, and larger. By the time we arrived at Kongsberg, it was a completely urban landscape. Nothing screamed 'Norway' at me. Oslo Sentrum wasn't all that different than Pittsburgh, or Washington D.C. at first glance. I put the scenery aside as I stepped off the train. As I looked around for Einar, the friend I went to see, I caught a glimpse of a tall, blonde haired man standing behind a pillar. I took a few steps back, and got a good look at my friend for the first time in ten years. "Einar!" I exclaimed. His slender, sculpted face lit up. We approached each other, and he embraced me with his 6'0" tall, 170 lb. frame. The short sides, and long hair on the top of his head painted a portrait of my friend which I was not familiar with. It was an expression of an individual traveling through time. People change. I just wondered if the new haircut personified any differences that have developed in my friend's *personality* over the past decade.

In 2005 Einar came to my high school in western PA as a foreign exchange student. He grew up in Trondheim, the third largest city in Norway. I was a senior and he was a junior. During our time together, we became best friends. I showed him much hospitality, inviting him into my home and taking him outdoors. I guided him in the culture of the Laurel Highlands of the Appalachian Mountains. We hiked and trout fished in the mountains. We went out to eat. He even attended the great bon fire party the evening of our graduation. I became his chauffeur. We developed an affinity for each other, and he was so pleased and impressed with the care I showed him that he wished one day he could repay the favor. So ten years later, as soon I had the time and money to make the trip, I went to see Einar for the summer solstice in Norway. The Midnight Sun.

I could feel a slight hesitation within him as we hugged and greeted each other. I figured there would be a gap to bridge, but I tried not to let it be apparent in my thoughts, speech, or body language. If he felt my love, I would feel his. I dove into stories about life since we had seen each other last, as we walked through the still-sleeping streets of central Oslo. I wanted a cigarette, but couldn't find my lighter. As we stood on a bridge which Einar pointed out to be the central location of most drug deals in that part of Oslo, he said "We'll wait here. Someone will have a lighter." In less than 30 seconds a man approached us. He was in his mid 20's. Einar thought he was Polish. I thought he was Russian. The man could have been from anywhere in between. He saw me pull a smoke from the red box of Pall Mall, and offered to buy one cigarette. I said if he could give me a light, he could have a cigarette, no charge. He was willing to pay me a dollar, and I was surprised that he figured the transaction should happen in American currency. Maybe that's the mode in Europe? American currency for street-transactions. I didn't get enough exposure to such to make any hard and fast decisions about the topic. The man had on a winter coat, and a knapsack on his back. From the look of his appearance, teeth and all, he had been living on the street. I told him and Einar the story of some friends and I sneaking into a music festival through Cheat Canyon one year. It was the one about me almost falling off a 300 foot rock face. I felt the urge to be loud and proud. I was sleep deprived, and needed to be all balls for a few minutes to stay alive. Reflecting on strengths and accomplishments has always been a personal way of staying focused and driven. Whatever is brewing in the mind usually has a way of being expelled into external actions. I needed it. The cigarette helped me ride the wave after the conversation ended with the Slavic man. We continued towards the apartment where we would be staying for the night (and where Einar had spent the night prior). The layout of streets wound about the gentle topography, narrow and cobblestone. Einar talked about the beggars and immigrants as we walked the ghetto. I don't know if I'd call the locale the ghetto, but then again I had no intimate relationship with the place, just as a passersby wouldn't call my last neighborhood in Morgantown the ghetto, at a glance. A ghetto may have been a stretch from the truth, maybe just in relativity. But they *did* light my dumpster on fire one night. There, the architecture was not particularly Scandinavian, but, then again I had little idea of what would be Scandinavian, especially in a ghetto. Buildings were three or four stories tall, often made of concrete, and painted neutral colors.

Finally we passed through the gate at Erik's apartment building and walked through the courtyard. I felt absorbed of European living; walls all around a small, brick, yard. The courtyard was quiet, spacious, and secluded. It was unique in appearance compared to the other buildings around, and nothing spoke cookie-cutter qualities of the neighborhood. Different than Pittsburgh. Einar buzzed Erik. The door opened and we walked up a flight of stairs. Einar and I sat in the living room of the apartment for a few moments. Beer cans were strewn about the coffee table. It felt like Saturday morning inn Oslo. The "L" shape of the room connected the kitchen to the living room. A novel face and body entered the room. Auburn hair capped the square, sculpted face of a somewhat shorter man with broad shoulders for his height. It was Erik. Einar and Erik went to elementary school together. When I heard the both of them speak in English (snikke de engelst) I could hear the subtlties of a Norwegian accent. "Sleep" I thought. No, that was reserved for the wee hours of the morning! I dropped my bag and we hit the streets running.

Erik knew the city better than Einar. One man lived in that city, and the other never ventured far out of the neighborhood of the apartment. Either way, the day had begun and we were on foot discovering Oslo. Erik was the kind of guy you wish to show you around. He knew the city well, and had a sense of pride about living there. I think that's where the word pride comes from, a sense of communal energy. He wanted to deliver as much joy and splendor as the city had to offer. Some of that would come from the unknown, the spontaneous generation of the spirit as it brewed and culminated from within the streets, and walls, and people. We started along a paved trail along the elv (river) running through town. Houses were built tight against the water's edge, reinforced with wood around the foundation. It kind of looked like something you'd see in Venice. The buildings were not new by any means, maybe 50, maybe 100, maybe 200 years old, but they were in good maintenance.

People cared for the quaint, peculiar parts of the city that had character intrinsic to the locale. Continuing along the path, we passed under bridges and through tunnels as we made our way back to the streets. We wove between the city blocks along the cobblestone streets. The foreign newness of the city left me lost. I couldn't conceive any particular direction, but slowly, we made our way to the market. As we got closer, you could hear music, and foot-traffic, and the soft hum of chatter from the modest crowd cruising the market mid-Saturday morning. The spirit of the city seemed to beat on an even meter as people, bicycles, and cars approached and passed. We breached a point were no motor vehicles were allowed, and the market quickly appeared before us. The tone of the city's spirit was mellow, and its texture was slightly gritty like sand softly sifting through the fingers. The market hummed with soft music from acoustic guitars, and vendors unintrusively advertised their products. Tents strung the length of the street we found ourselves on, stretching for half a mile until the street met the city park. Sustainable apparel and accessories, organic health foods, and not-so-organic or healthy foods were being bought and sold from the tents. Erik received a free burlap handbag from a vendor, and shortly thereafter, we found ourselves in one of Oslo's many parks. The park and the market had a positive energy. To call it bubbly would be a stretch, but spirit was rising and receding, ebbing and flowing. The market was romantic, and handsome, but we were in search of strong drink. We casually put distance between ourselves and the market in search of coffee. I was finishing my second cigarette of the morning about two or three blocks away from the park when we found a café` that met Erik's approval. The place sat on the corner. There was no exclamation in the *place's* sign. The interior was fitted with a bakery counter and one table. I sat at a table outside as Erik and Einar went in to buy coffee.

The beautiful blonde wearing sunglasses sitting adjacent held my interest more tightly than the black drink. Her name was Helena (Helaina). I began casual conversation with Helena. She spoke excellent English and delivered an energy that was tranquil yet confident. All that needed to be known was known. There was no sense of urgency. There were no pressing feelings of desire. Not from me to her, certainly not her to me, and neither either of us about the world around us. I figured all the impression, significance, and enlightenment would come just as time meant for it to be delivered. But, there was sincere interest between us as we sat and talked, almost preoccupied with time and space. I could feel her embracing the day as many seemed to do in Norway. Einar and Erik returned with coffee, and a glass of water for each of us. I drank two glasses of water. Helena left, and the three of us sat at the café talking, and not talking. I was in a somber state of mind from the lack of sleep. My eyes weren't as heavy as I imagined they would be, but cigarettes felt like a necessary catalyst. My friends' voices and engagement helped propel one waking moment into the next. That felt like "first social contact." Strange women. How shrewd! How brilliant! Einar and Erik let Helena and I go about the acquaintance, and afterward I felt bright rising faith in what I had come to do. Live!

We finished our coffee and water, and rose to our feet. The streets rose up to meet us like a welcoming host opening its door to adventure and investigation. It was still too early for beer, or was it? We began moving in a direction different from that which we came, and before long we found ourselves at a grocery store. The coffee was not enough to satisfy thirst. The aisles in the grocery store were tight and the advertising was minimal. It was no American supermarket. Einar bought a bottle of water for me and a drink for himself, and Erik got something to drink. We went through the tight checkout, and Einar made humorous small talk with the cashier. After we left he asked if I noticed anything different in their dialects. There was a difference in the length of pronounced vowels, and the hardness of consonants much like the difference between pittsburghese in comparison with proper American English. From that point on I paid little attention to accents. My major challenge was isolating spoken words within phrases. All foreign languages seem to pose that problem upon initial exposure. Phrases and sentences sound like one long word. It's intimidating and impossible to learn the language until you gain enough comfort and experience so that you can identify where one word begins and the other ends. There was no demand for me to learn Norsk, although part of me wishes there was. I would have felt a little more shock, and would have been drawn out of my comfort zone if everyone was speaking a foreign language. But, damn near everyone spoke English, and spoke it extremely well. I was truly impressed how well Norwegians could explain deep, complex ideas in their *second* language. I felt jealous, and a little short-changed by my own culture. The flux of cultures flowing through the Laurel Highlands is slightly less than that of Oslo, but the principle of my argument is no less valid. You will meet people in your life who do not speak your language, and you will probably be required to communicate with those people. There are other ways of communicating than just using spoken words. In Norway, children are taught English beginning in first grade. At that age, the minds are more open and malleable than they are later in life. American students are not exposed to a second language until high school. Sad. The ability to share time and ideas is restricted greatly by only knowing a single language. It's like wearing the blinders. Much of other cultures are closed off by the lack of fluency in other languages. It pours over to feeling comfortable around people different than you. Communicating takes on a new definition when you have that ability. Back to the trip.

We navigated the gentle topography across Oslo. Hills lifted in height with variable relief and we trotted the rolling slopes half a kilometer at a time passing fountains and parks, and an outdoor karaoke stage that also served beer. Erik thought it would be a good idea to grab a brew, but Einar couldn't wait to put some distance between us and that place. There were a group of women onstage, probably in their 20's and 30's, strapped in the appearance of a bachelorette party. It was still morning. People were drinking, but we walked on to look for beer elsewhere as I lit another cigarette. We walked aimlessly. Nothing looked familiar, but the city did not feel alien. There was something very comforting about Oslo. There was no pressure. It did not demand anything of you like other large cities I've been too. Instead, the day leisurely unfolded without a desired destination or any preconceived conceptions of where and how it should end. Oslo and its people knew the end would come as it may, and when it does, they would enjoy it for whatever it may be worth. I was interested in what I might find, but I was not filled with frenzied curiosity. Maybe the sleep deprivation helped that motion.

As we walked, I noticed lots of beautiful women passing without a long void in the interval. It excited desire, and gave hope to the possibilities superficial intimacy. I let it die as a sight seen as I continued with the rhythm we were in. We wandered as the pretty women passed, and I just followed Erik. Pace and complement. Sensual desires were overshadowed by the enjoyment of sharing intelligent conversations. I think privately, that was the whole point of the trip, to be able to share ideas with a person in a foreign environment, and for that I was in good company. My friends were intelligent, opinionate, and open-minded. Erik and Einar both spent considerable time in Asia and throughout Europe. Erik lived in Germany for about a year, and Einar Italy. I *was* able to share ideas. I found an opportunity to share my thoughts about what I believed spirit to be, and how it had a singular divine source. I was surprised how well my friends accepted and validated my ideas despite living in a primarily atheist country. A person's beliefs doesn't inhibit their ability to harmonize. That capability lies in the ability to maintain focus on what's coming at you and reflect upon that from the heart. Erik was like a sponge. He listened attentively as I explained simplified ideas of spiritually and metaphysics. And when he responded he was engaged and interested. I was beginning to like the guy.

To contrast my stance on spirituality, we arrived a park, Vigeland Sculpture Park. The place had a wide walkway lined with dozens of ten-foot-tall nude sculptures of men, women, and children. Some were individual bodies, some coupled with other bodies, in a variety of poses. I wasn't at completely at peace with the place, but found a little erotic humor about it. The statues were tasteful and displayed life and activity in variety. I wondered how exposure to such a place would affect a child or young person's view on nudity and sexuality. Comfort could be gained, but what measure of morality would be lost? It was all about taste, respect and patience; the adversity to the perverse. Erik and Einar found a lot of humor in Vigeland Park. They talked me into posing with the sculptures for pictures, and before we exited I was squatting behind a male statue, cupping its balls. The far end of the exhibit was punctuated with a 25 foot tall tower sculpted of naked bodies stacked and woven about each other. The tower of sex may have been the one thing that sacrificed reality. That was Einar's object of attention. Otherwise, everything brought together a face of God and humanity that is real, and often ignored in America and American society, the provision of sex. Deprivation from that spirit is capable of driving souls away from reality, but excess of such an indulgence specializes one's way of life. Despite Vigeland Park, tension never grew.

As we left the statues behind, and continued through the park, Einar asked my opinion of Oslo, and its people. The morning was refreshing. I was able to take my deep breaths and move in time with its folks. My friends were buddies. Jolly all the way. They let me make the first handshakes and guided me along when I didn't know which way to go. The light and the air spread the feel. The energy between those hearts and myself crossed its interfaces with natural conductivity. I said it was relaxed. It felt like a recurring theme. There was disregard for material consumption. The Norsk gave off a vibe that spoke ignorance to all the pointless shit in life. It could be heard in their clear, energetic voices. It could be heard in their language as they spoke in a smooth, romantic, northern tongue. We began to develop interest in beer; strong desire without a sense of urgency. The day unfolded on its own gradual terms, and we consumed it as it delivered itself to us. I smoked a cigarette as Erik led us to Highbury Bar with only a general idea of its location. The beautiful girls with their shapely bodies passed like an inexhaustible resource. Just as one moved out of sight, another would appear.

Eventually we made it to Highbury Bar. There were roughly 10 or 12 tables sitting below a canopy on the patio that recessed into the ground. Only two or three tables were occupied. We made our way to the edge of the patio and sat in the sunlight. The small, black table-tops were made from wire-mesh. Erik and Einar sat on the bench that was built into the concrete barrier bordering the patio. A waiter quickly came and delivered menus. Beer was the primary demand, but we were all beginning to feel hungry by that hour. It was around 3:30 in the afternoon, and we had been walking all day. Einar and I had a quick conversation about the thirst quenching capabilities IPA's. Crisp, cool, and refreshing. He asked if I liked the style of brew, and suggested I order the Norgne "Two Captains" IPA. The beer had a light hoppy flavor compared to Goose Island or Green Flash. It had hints of fruitiness, not piney or floral. The flavor profile was a good fit for the warm

Oslo day. Definitely a refreshing beer, and being delivered in 1 liter bottles at 9% alcohol by volume, I had a bit of a jag on after my first bottle. Then we ordered pizzas. Einar said they were most likely frozen and reheated. I thought the food was good.

Sometime while we were eating, Erik's girlfriend arrived. She was pretty with red hair, freckles, and wide hips. Her name was Amy. She was born in England, and spoke with an English accent despite living in Oslo for the past 14 years. Her and Erik were busy asking me questions about writing while I tried to eat. I took bites of pizza while they asked questions, and I answered them with mouthfuls of food. The food was great and I was starving. A reading group Amy was part of rested the challenge of writing a haiku on its members. Amy challenged me to produce the words for the poem.

"If these shoes could talk-

They would tell you where I've been-

May the road greet you."

The words felt in place, but it was not the first time they crossed my mind. Years prior while working on the Ohio River I thought about the story my shoes would tell if they could talk; the places they've been, the textures they have tromped upon. How would their tales of my travels differ from the words of my own mouth? After we finished the poem I was able to eat the rest of my pizza, then I ordered a coffee porter. Einar ordered a liter of Two Captains for himself.

The porter was good. It's hard to screw up a coffee porter or coffee stout. The grains and beans the brews are steeped with have been roasted so dark that they overpower any foulness in the coffee or beer. All that can be tasted is the coffee profile. We finished our beers, then Einar and I walked inside the bar to watch a futbol game while Erik and Amy stayed outside on the patio talking for a while. The bar was dark inside. Dim lighting showed the face of mangy wood work. Gnarl and burl flustered the loss of light within the establishment. Leather benches and wooden chairs lined an empty, chaotic room filled with short tables. I ordered a Ringnes, a run-of-the-mill Norwegian beer, and a shot of Jameson. The Ringnes reminded me of I.C. Light or Keystone. There were no popping flavors, just a simple, somewhat watered-down taste of barley and hops. I don't remember what futbol teams were playing on TV. We caught the last 15 minutes of the game then the four of us left Highbury Bar. As we did, Amy left. Then we were on our way to see where the king lives. We covered the city blocks with a nice beer-buzz in the head. It was less than 30 minutes until we arrived at the palace. "Palace" is the only word I can use to describe the place. The building was nothing like the castles of old I have seen in Great Britain or Ireland. There was no fancy architecture. The walls were smooth and flat between the modest pillars that stood between each column of windows. A soldier guarded a statue outside. There was no fence around the building. The place was pretty low key. In a few moments I had seen all there was to see from the outside. We continued in the same general direction enroute to the marina. Before long we were seaside.

A finger of sea water reached inland to the city of Oslo creating a fjord. The fjord was not the amazingly majestic reaches of sea bordered by sheer rock cliffs ascending hundreds of feet on either side of the water that you see in pictures. No, this reach of sea was a bit more modest. Hills and small mountains could be seen rising to the sky on the opposite side of the water, but climbing gear wasn't necessary to step foot on the docks. Roughly ten acres of water were occupied by boats with wooden docks spreading over the water in a ganglion pattern. Big boats, little boats, sail boats, motor boats all docked in the fjord. The airy clarity of the ocean blew inland from the water. The gentle smell of salt, and a slightly more pungent smell of fish filled the air. The horizon stretched out far and let the mind wander and imagine the possibilities should one sneak away from the bounds of land and set sail on the open ocean. The restaurants and buildings stood handsomely against the backdrop of the marina. Large foot-streets and tall glass buildings, or chic patios spoke tones of elegance, and a progressive market-economy. Comfortable western living was visible in the marina. Einar spoke to me about sustainable development of the area. That was his profession.

    He had a bachelor's of science in construction engineering, and worked for the government designing building permits that incorporated sustainable building construction and energy use. He talked about skylights, the angle of windows and solar panels, and triple paned windows that had special tint. It sounded very impressive, and made me wonder if we have such programs in America. There are subsidies for energy and agriculture in our country, but I have never heard of such innovations with building construction. If changes could be created in that demand, that might be the only way we could see changes in the way we produce a supply of sustainable infrastructure. The heart of the problem must be dissolved at the source. The source is apparently the desire from within the human consumer. Norway seemed quite progressive, but when I expressed awe to Einar, he told me even the best countries are SEVEN years behind the technology being developed and implemented in Germany. Research and development was a big part of sustainable construction. Supporting the sale of such technology seemed good, and to me that was its initial and final impact on the economy, but I was wrong. Einar went on to talk about how supporting such technology creates a demand for progression. When people see how the government helps companies who provide sustainable building products and practices, more people become interested in developing new ways of saving energy and resources. That development creates more jobs in R&D. A broader spectrum of resources appears at the surface. And, in that way progression becomes perpetual because there is a real demand for it. Meanwhile, the implementation and construction efforts do not fall victim to the tragedies of risk involved with new technology, because the government is fronting the bill for the difference in cost between conventional construction and cutting-edge, sustainable construction.

After a few deep breaths of salty air, and gentle breeze in our faces, we made our way to our next destination, a small stadium with a big-screen (20 feet by 20 feet) televising a futbol game. The European Cup futbol tournament was taking place while I was in Norway. It's like a smaller version of World Cup with about 12 teams in the competition. It was a pretty big deal. Norway was not competing this year, but we were making a trip a few kilometers from the marina to the stadium to see Iceland take on Belgium. Projector and big-screen would be the technology for observation as that seemed like the preferred medium while I was in country. I was getting tired along the way, and my perception was beginning to become dull from the lack of sleep. We arrived at the stadium, and took seats at ground level. My eyes were getting heavy, then out of nowhere Einar showed up with a pint of Carlsberg for me. The beer hit my flavor and olfactory senses and I began to wake. Erik and Einar laughed at my tired head as it paid more attention to the women walking past than the match between Iceland and Belgium. Everyone in the stadium was rooting for Iceland. Einar explained that they are something of a little brother of Norway, an island settled by Vikings. He also explained that the population is so small and isolated that someone developed and app to avoid sexual contact with unknown family members for those living on the small island. I got a chuckle out of that. It made me think about a liberty I never before considered, living in a country such as America, the freedom to flirt.

Anyway, the Carlsberg woke me up a bit, and by the time I finished the pint I was getting hungry again. I went to the concession stand to see what food they had. There was a sign that said "Hot Dogs" and a price was given, but I can't accurately remember what that was. I ordered a "hot dog" and a pint of Carlsberg. They served me a plate. There were two grilled wieners, one red, one brown, German potato salad, with a spicy mustard and onions, and a small piece of bread. I was thrilled! I started on the red hot dog. It was spicy and delicious. As I neared the end of it, I thought, "Maybe I should eat the brown one now so my last bite of meat will be this delicious, red frankfurter." So I ate the brown one, finished the red one, and moved onto the potato salad. The potato salad was delicious. I never ate potato salad with that exact character. The food had the spice of the soul, from the ground, from the people. I only had German potato salad once before, and it had no onions, nor the spicy mustard mixed into the oil and vinegar dressing. I sat there drinking my beer with a full tummy, and watched the end of the futbol game. It ended in a tie, and everyone was a little disappointed. I would have loved to see the place erupt had Iceland won. I could only imagine such a victorious environment in Europe. I suppose that's the reason for all the excitement. Seeing the home country actually win and not just lose or tie is quite rare. The tournament only happens once every four years. The heritage of the game is at a pinnacle in Europe. And, there is so much patriotism that a victory is more than just a win in a sporting event. It's jubilation of the fighting spirit of a nation!

After the game, we made our way back to Erik's apartment to shower and get ready for the night. I made it to the shower before either of my friends did. Cold water. That was the only way I was going to stay awake. I scrubbed the crustiness off and lathered my hair. Then I shaved around my beard, put on clean clothes and sat on the couch. After being awake and on the go for such a long time, the practice in personal hygiene felt incredible! I sat up on Erik's couch and talked with him as Einar occupied the shower. A phone call from a group of girls started us on a conversation about relationships.

He began talking about how much sex a person can have in a European city, and the endless supply of beautiful women, but explained how vacuous the game can become. After a while the pleasure from sex loses its zest, and the pinnacle of stimulation feels a bit dull. He continued that eventually a meaningful relationship becomes more satisfying than sex, although sex is an important part of that relationship. It's a sustainable comfort of the sensual sort. Some humans like myself reside on the transcendental end of the spectrum instead of the sensual. Whoring was something I had a tough time relating to although Erik wasn't really a whore. But still, whatever the comforting complement may be, man needs someone to share the journey of life with.

I explained my position, one that involves great personal freedom with a great deal of time devoted to reading, writing, and trying to learn new languages. I enjoy recreation like kayaking, fishing, and personal seclusion in the forest in acts of hunting and lone-hiking. I told Erik that I would have a hard time sacrificing those things as well as the freedom of an independent future, with hopes of, at the time, of earning a PhD and executing research in remote, exotic locations. Sharing income and financial responsibilities creates tumultuous atmosphere in relationships. That was something I did not want. I would avoid it at all costs. Erik appreciated what I had to say, but he made a statement that put an impact on my mind. He said eventually, everyone needs affection, and a person to share the journey with. I agreed with him. Without others, nothing is worthwhile. I saw that immediately that first day in Norway. I could have seen all that I saw in Oslo by myself, but it would have meant little to nothing had I seen it alone. More fun is had when others are with you.

During that conversation, I told Erik I do have something of a girlfriend, but there is no affection, nor expectation of commitment. A partner is not anything the follows any declared boundaries. It is felt in the connection. My girl and I were not emotionally responsible for the other. All there really was between us was dinner every-other week, but she was pretty, she was a she, and had positive energy. When we had dinner together we could talk about anything. I could dive into the depths of my mind and she could deliver hers. She was intelligent, and that is the sexiest trait of all. It was alone time with another person, someone who held the prospects of life to be shared.

Einar vacated the bathroom, an Erik showered. I laid back on the couch and closed my eyes for a second and fell asleep for five minutes. Way too easily. Einar spoke to me and I woke up. It was close to 11 o'clock and the dark of night was beginning to fall. Erik, now clean, had gotten dressed, and I put on my boots. That raised alarm to my Norwegian friends. They said a lot of night clubs don't let in men with boots, but we'd give it a try. When we arrived at the club, it wasn't my boots that rubbed the bouncer the wrong way. It was my eyes. The bouncer asked if I had been drinking all day. I had been, but I didn't feel drunk. I felt tired. I told him I had been awake, traveling for the past 38 hours. My appeal was worthless. They didn't let us in, so Erik proposed we go to the rocker bar nearby. By now the darkness of night had completely fallen. The initial interest of setting sail to that particular time and place, Norway in late June, was to see the midnight sun. Such a phenomenon is only visible above 66 degrees latitude, north or south. I was at approximately 60 degrees north latitude in Oslo. Sunlight and the length of day hold many powers over the mind and spirit. In my head I had a mystical attraction to see 24 hours of daylight. I had no hypothesis or forecast to what I might find, but that first night in Oslo was dark. I had expected it. It was too far south. The sun only stays in the sky for 24 hours above the Arctic Circle, and Oslo was in the south of the country.

Anyway, it was dark. We were on our way to the rocker bar. I had boots on. The night had an eerie, creeping flow. Everything seemed to move with the pace and rhythm that was present in the morning when we first set out on the street, but now the continuity that daylight brought had faded. Still, you could see the spirit and energy of the city coming from miles away. It was a casual pace steeped with intrigue and interest. The soft glow of fluorescent light invited souls to roam with random destinations presenting themselves just as they became afoot. The rocker bar was just that. Rock and roll played over the stereo, hinting vibrations through the front door. The bouncer was almost my height, long hair with a beer belly. He made no comments of my appearance or condition when we entered. He looked at my passport (it was easier to prevent losing it if I kept the thing under watch, close to my body at all times) and I walked in. The whole place was built of wood that became well-seasoned over the years. Einar and Erik bought stouts, and I ordered a draft of Pilsner Urquell, a Czech pilsner. The tap was impressive, complicated with knobs and levers, all wood and brass. When the beer began flowing for the third time that day, the effect remained in-character. We sat at a table close to the door, with my chair looking out onto the main street. Conversation was quiet at first, I could feel myself starting to succumb to the lack of sleep. Then, some cock-rock came over the stereo, and I remembered Phil, the man I share much life-history with and the man who loves telling jokes in bars (horrible ones sometimes). I pulled a favorite of mine to tell Erik and Einar. "It's a teenage boys birthday, and he's walking past a hotel with his duck, and a hooker says 'hey boy wanna fuck?' The boy says sure but all I have is this duck. The hooker says well I guess that will work for payment. So they fuck, then the hooker says 'that was so good, if you do it again I'll give you the duck back'. So they do it again, he gets his duck back and makes his way home. When the bus pulls up to the stop, the duck up and flies out of his arms and gets run over. The bus driver says 'sorry kid, all I can give you for the duck is two dollars.' So the kid takes the money and when he gets home, his dad asks how his day was and the kid replies 'Pretty good. I got a fuck for a duck, a duck for a fuck, and two bucks for a fucked up duck.'" Erik and Einar enjoyed the joke and that got things flowing. I got loud, and started expressing the size of my balls through stories. When I talk about the day I did LSD on the Upper Gauley, I like the whole room to hear. Its vain and egotistical, I know. But, it's an expression of character, and if I can make a room more vibrant by an expression of personality, I feel I have the duty to do so. The bar started to fill up, and really come alive. Rock and roll types, dudes that approached the realm of hipster, and a few fashionable individuals occupied the joint. The bar was raunchy. It laid somewhere between the realm of punk and hipster, and all I wanted to do was roll up my sleeves and puff on some smoke. The bartenders were kept busy with the crowd, and I was having a great time. This was the kind of place I was hoping to end up; a place where I could speak with testicular fortitude, and not offend anyone.

Well it seemed that way. It seemed I had not offended anyone. I was trying to inspire a bit of my attitude in the people who shared the same immediate environment. After my second Pilsner Urquell, I needed some nicotine. I burned through an entire pack of cigarettes through the course of the day, and I wanted 'just one more.' I walked out to the small lot that lead back to an alley where a half-dozen people were standing there, smoking. I bummed a smoke and bummed a light. And before I could finish the square, the company left. There was one man. The boy was in his early twenties and dressed fashionably. He approached me and said "Hey man, I'm not gonna try to fuck with you, or anything, but do you wanna take a walk with me?" I said no. "Are you trying to fuck everything up?" he asked. I said no. "You're fucking everything up!" I replied with an indifferent, "Oh." The boy stormed off. Maybe this was 'his' bar, and I was some loud mouth American that rubbed him the wrong way. I was really too tired give a shit, so I walked back inside after finishing the cigarette. The bouncer stopped me along the way and said I should drink some water, I looked dehydrated. I stated my case of how long I had been awake, and he made no argument, only repeated that I should drink some water. So, to appease the man, I did. I told Einar the whole story when I sat back down. He said the boy wanted to fight me for God knows why, and laughed about the bouncer saying I looked dehydrated. "I don't know what's with that guy? He's keeps telling everyone they look dehydrated!" Einar's voice was full of humor and amusement. I finished my water, and told my friends I needed to get home. If I had one more beer I would be sleeping in the bar. I had as much confrontation as I could afford, being sleep deprived and in a foreign country. It was time to sleep. We had a morning flight to Trondheim the next day. Einar went with me back to the apartment, and Erik stayed out chasing the night. We walked along the river as we made our way back to the apartment, affording the opportunity to take a piss away from the public eye. Einar and I yammered on about nothing the whole way. And as soon as my back hit the couch I was out.

Day 2:

No sooner did I fall asleep, the alarm on my phone went off. It was 7:30 AM Sunday. We had a 10:00 AM flight to Trondheim. I packed my bag, and Einar and I were off to the train to take us to the airport. The twenty minute train ride from Oslo Sentrum to Oslo Flygplats passed with anticipation, at least for me. We arrived, and when we got our boarding passes, something caught Einar's eye. He looked up at the monitor. The 10 AM flight into Trondheim had been canceled. Panic ran through my veins instantly. Einar stayed collected. He knew a few flights ran between Oslo and Trondheim daily. We walked over to personnel for assistance. We got new boarding passes. Einar's flight was at 2 PM and mine was at 3. Nothing to do, but wait, or so I thought. Heavy drinking from the night before left my stomach doing strange things, so I bought a chicken tikka baguette. The spicy sauce caught my eye, but didn't sit comfortably in my belly. I munched away, and Einar bought passes for both of us into Scandinavian Airlines' lounge. I thought it peculiar; I had no problem waiting at our gate for a few hours. The airport wasn't too crowded that Sunday morning. It was far more comfortable than Pittsburgh, and especially Newark. We walked upstairs and onto the lounge. Free beer, free juice, free water, free food. I soon regretted deciding on the chicken tikka. Oatmeal and Carlsberg would have been a better choice. Einar downed five pints of Carlsberg before we left the lounge. My stomach settled down enough for me to develop an appetite for beer, and I had a few pints. That seemed to grease my stomach quite well. We left the lounge sometime after noon, and walked about to kill some time. The international terminal was filling with life. There were people from all over crowding around the shops, Europeans, Americans, Asians, Norwegian soldiers. Thankfully, the terminal wasn't a circus with activity. I got another baguette (ham, mozzarella, and oregano this time) with the $20 voucher the airline gave us for the canceled flight. We walked back to gates 14 and 15 where we were to board. It was a little after 1:00. Einar and I sat quietly next to the large plate-glass window. Across from us sat two Swedish pilots. I silently interpreted the words I could. I learned a very meagre portion of Swedish before I left. Einar said the two languages were similar, and I didn't find any Norwegian language software before my trip. I entertained myself with the challenge for about half an hour. They kept repeating the word "bil," car. Then when the pilots walked away Einar asked me, "Could you tell those men were Swedish?" I told him yes, and an honest smile of excitement grew on his face.

From the moment Einar found out I was trying to learn Swedish, he was thrilled. He was impressed with the fact that I wasn't going to sit back, and take advantage of the fact that the entire country spoke English as well or almost as well as they spoke Norsk. Yes, learning language gained respect from my host, but I did it for me, for my experience. I hoped to be able to listen to Norwegians speak their native tongue. I wanted a feel for how they explained their thoughts and feelings in their own language. I wanted to feel the connection between observation and explanation of the folks hosting me. I was chasing the feel brought on by perception and verbage. I wanted an intimate sensation of Norway. Unfortunately I fell short, and that moment in the airport was the closest I came to my goal. I didn't have a fluent understanding of Swedish, and furthermore, Norwegian and Swedish were not as similar as I assumed when Einar said the two are similar. Maybe the language was, but the accent was not. Maybe I was lost, primarily, in the delivery of Norwegian. Yeah! That's a good excuse!

Soon Einar boarded his plane, and I came dangerously close to falling asleep in the airport that afternoon. After opening heavy eyes sometime after 2:30 I addressed the personal responsibility of staying awake and catching my flight. That moment struck when you realize you are waking from slumber and you may or may not have missed a responsibility. If I would have needed to get another passage to Trondheim, things would have gotten complicated. There would be plenty of time to sleep come Monday morning. Another ten minutes passed, and my flight began boarding. The weather in Oslo was beautiful. The sunlight felt warm as it came through the glass while I walked out the gangway. I walked onto the plane expecting a small aircraft. There were three rows of seats on each side of the center aisle. I had never been on a plane of that particular size before. I had a window seat. There was a delay in our take-off on account of lost baggage. As we waited for the airline to find the bag, I watched a large bug repeatedly fly over the wing of the plane, fall on to the wing, squirm on its back, fall off, then begin buzzing around again. I thought it strange, the routine. It continued for nearly all of the 20 minutes we were delayed.

The flight took off, and I tried to get comfortable as we cruised at altitude. I relaxed, just enough. Within an hour the pilot came over the speaker and said we would be beginning the descent to land. I looked out my window at the Norwegian countryside once we dropped below the clouds. Tall narrow, houses, different than American ranch-houses, farmhouses, and Victorian houses, bordered the farms that filled the gentle topography below the hills and mountains of western Norway. The topography was characteristic of glaciated, lowland, landscape. Wide, gently-sloping land undulated across the low ground. The peaks were too sporadic, too disconnected to create valleys, but the peaks were not limited in quantity. Most only rose a few hundred feet, but in the distance towards the east, I could see great mountains rising high into the sky, showing prominence of thousands of feet. Small lakes were spotted into the lowlands. The landscape reminded me of the Adirondacks, and it was the first time I was able to compare Alpine-glaciated landscapes. Similar arrangements of matter, and similar forces of energy, will produce similar results. Uniformitarianism at its finest.

The plane descended. My heart began to race a bit. All I could see below me was houses and streets. There was no runway insight. The landing strip was so close to the community that I thought we were about to make an emergency landing on a city street, but as he continued down, the asphalt appeared below the plane just in time. The plane reached the port, and we exited the gangway in light rain. I walked to baggage claim where Einar was waiting for me. "How was the landing?" He asked with a grin. I told him I was nervous. I didn't see the runway until we were almost on the ground. He laughed and commented that if the plane comes from the other direction, it looks like you are about to crash into the fjord when you land. My bag appeared on the carousel quickly. We grabbed it and walked out to the bus, bought boarding passes, and climbed aboard.

The weather was dreary as the bus approached the city of Trondheim along highways, through tunnels, and around roundabouts. I could see small mountain peaks with much steeper sides than the mountains of western Pennsylvania. Faces of igneous rock were exposed and bordered by conifers. Hemlocks, firs, and spruces provided structure and shelter over steep, mossy hillsides. Rivers and creeks carved their way into the ground. The soil looked thin, and that was apparent in the vegetation and hydrology. The cool temperatures and small range of seasonal variation prevented rock from weathering to thick soils. Shallow root systems that were adapted to quickly draining soils supported the trees and mosses. The creeks followed bedrock that lacked chaotic, angular jointing like that found in sedimentary mountains. Instead, the paths of the creeks in Norway were more linear, and revealed intense down-cutting as the water moved over the rocks. The rivers were wide and wound about, following the larger valleys carved out by the glaciers, and eventually flowed into Trondheimsfjord. Twenty minutes after departing from the airport, we were in the city of Trondheim. Einar hit the button to alert the driver we wanted to get off.

We grabbed my bag and stepped onto the sidewalk. I had to tie one of my bootlaces, and adjust my pack a little bit so the first impression and the immediate impression would be slightly different. Once I was upright and walking, I began taking in the atmosphere. The way the suite fits will focus the eye the way God sees fit. The bus dropped us off in a residential section, mostly apartments. The concrete buildings and houses with wooden siding hung above the narrow asphalt streets and wide asphalt sidewalks. Young trees bordered the road, and cars were parked perpendicular to the flow of traffic. Einar pointed to the end of the first side-street we came to, and said that is where he grew up. I was excited to see if I could identify a connection of who he is and where he is from. I had the better part of a week to feel the energy of Trondheim, and interpret the consciousness derived by it. I took my time and enjoyed the vacant dreary streets for the duration of our walk.

Two blocks down the street, we changed direction. The houses developed a more foreign feel as we walked deeper into town. Their foundations were rather square, and most of the houses were painted red, white, or yellow. Einar talked about the demographics of the city, and how it attracted scientists and writer. Trondheim was one of the original intellectual cities of Norway, and Europe for that matter. I was busy taking in the sights, sounds, and smells of the city. The fjord reached in to the bottom of the city where it met the river, Nidelva. The skies and light precipitation held a maritime calmness about the city. The tone of Trondheim was muffled in that moment, but felt capable of breathing a warm, sensual breath on the neck of anyone in that place at that time. We walked on, and I continued to make the acquaintance of the foreign neighborhood. It was new and had a subtle romance about it.

After a long walk uphill, we reached Einar's apartment complex. There were two buildings, one four stories tall, the other five stories tall. They occupied half a city block with a courtyard between the two. We walked to the door, he punched in the code, we took the elevator up four floors, he unlocked his door and we walked in. The apartment was small. Einars bed was in a small room encased by sliding glass doors. There was a narrow gap at the foot of the bed to walk, and the queen mattress butted tight up the walls. I dropped my bag and stepped out onto the balcony. It was just large enough for a grill, two sun-beds, and small standing room. I looked north out onto the fjord. That misty atmosphere looked as though it might recede. I walked back in, and laid down on Einar's couch while he rustled dinner together. As I laid there Einar and I talked, and he tossed a book to me, "Vagabonding" by Rolf Potts. I began reading about the art of long term travel. Within the first few pages, I began thinking about travel in different terms. Rolf said that long-term travel is not something that takes an extravagant source of money. It's a lifestyle that takes know-how and self-control. Making small sacrifices in daily life, like not spending money on tobacco or coffee could supply you with enough money to see places and meet people in foreign lands for weeks even months. Unfortunately, the small indulgences like coffee and tobacco provide me with simple pleasures. That helps me get through the work day, and helps me enjoy working to the degree that I do. I only made it about forty pages into the book while I stayed with Einar. The book was intriguing, and cultivated an interest to read the words, and cognize the thoughts the whole way through until the end. Then maybe read it again, and again until I have gained as much as I can prior to the education provided by the experience of long-term travel.

The frozen spinach and fresh salmon sizzled on the induction stove-top, and I eased back into the couch. It felt good to kick my feet up after all the action that filled the past 57 hours. It was approaching 7 PM. Einar set the table, and served the food. We sat before a meal in an awkward silence, as if he secretly wanted me to say a prayer before we ate. Secretly, I wanted to say a blessing as well. He glanced up at me, then I asked. "Do mind if I say a blessing over our food before we eat?" He wore a simple smile of gratitude as if satisfied by my request. I prayed, "Dear Lord…" it began. I went on to give thanks for the sun that feeds the plants that feed us, and the waters that feed the fish that feed us. I finished, and we dug in. The salmon was seasoned with lemon-pepper and garlic. It was soft and flakey. The usual dryness of frozen salmon wasn't there. No, this was fresh from the rivers near Trondheim. The meat melted in the mouth. The flavor and aroma lacked the funkiness of packaged fish. The innate fishiness was still there. You could taste the oil of the salmon, but it was not pungent. The garlic and lemon pepper offered a good compliment of flavors to the meat. Savory, slightly spicy, and slightly tangy. I was unsure about the frozen spinach. During the cooking, the ice crystals around the greens melted, creating a more soggy version of the vegetable than the fresh, leafy spinach I'm used to. I helped myself to a small portion, and cracked some salt and pepper over the vegetables. The fresh cracked salt delivered seasoning that was strong yet subtle. The flavor could be tasted throughout, but there was no dryness or astringency as a result of the seasoning. Very little of the mineral was needed to achieve a splendid taste. The lentils were my least favorite of meal. The texture was the most appealing aspect of them, flesh wrapped in a soft cuticle. The flavor bland, but they felt good in the stomach. I helped myself to more spinach, and mixed it with the beans. Mixing the lentils and spinach made a nice taste/texture compliment. A little salt and pepper to season the pair as they went from plate, to fork, to mouth, and the meal was a great success. It was truly cuisine. Fine dining in a friend's home. He was no five-star-chef but he certainly knew what he was doing in a kitchen. Eating was the great prize. Everything was delicious, the salmon, lentils and spinach. I complimented Einar on dinner, and we talked about the food for a few minutes as I regained my position on the couch.

Clouds returned in the sky as they took on a darker shade of grey. That was the first complete meal I had had since Thursday. The hot dogs and potato salad at the futbol game was good like the pizza Saturday, but this was a true meal in the sense that kin know it as.

Thought, feeling, and effort was put in to preparing food. Thanks was given to the Creator, and neither daintiness nor savagery was expressed in the act of consuming the meal. After dinner settled in our bellies for a few minutes, we grabbed our coats, put our boots back on, and hit the streets. Earlier in the day Einar asked if I would like to go for a walk after dinner. I told him yes. I only had a short while in Norway, and I wanted to experience as much as I could. I know Sunday evenings at home are a sleepy hour. The day is spent at church, eating and relaxing, but before I turn in for the night and submit to the coming work week, I feel a bit of restlessness, and find a place for a heavy snack and a few beers, preferably with the company of a good friend or two.

    When we made it to the sidewalk, Einar asked how long of a walk I was interested in. I said roughly an hour and a half. "Perfect," was his reply. We started walking southwest. Foot streets intersected and led us past an elementary school on our way to a park. As we crossed a street traveled by motorcars and entered the park, Einar said the summer brings the people to the park to sun-bath and picnic. Not everyone in the city has the luxury of a deck or balcony to do those things in the comfort of their own home or apartment, so that leisure was found in the rolling grassy fields of the park which was dotted with trees. I looked to the top of the hill as Einar gestured in that direction, pointing to Kristiansten Fort. From the bottom of the hill I could see an old, whitewashed artillery garrison sitting above a heavy, concrete retaining wall twelve to fourteen feet tall, as the wall wrapped around the knoll. Einar just called it The Fort. We took the long way to the top of the hill and walked out to the west face.

Kristiansten Fort sat high above the city of Trondheim, and the west face was nearly vertical, dropping at least a hundred feet before meeting houses. Once inside the walls of Kristiansten Fort, ideas of defense and battle filled my head. There were prison quarters, lookouts, and artillery. Invasions from the sea could easily be spotted from the fort. It looked down onto the fjord from a bird's-eye-view. During World War II, Nazi Germany overtook the fort during their occupation of Norway. Norwegian Freedom-Fighters were kept prisoner in the dozen or so cells, highly exposed to the weather. The firing squad lined-up Norwegian prisoners in the center of the horseshoe of cells for execution, and a memorial was set in place for those who made the ultimate sacrifice once Kristiansten Fort was made a historical landmark. It was a minimalist military instillation. Cannon fire could reach far considering the fort's elevation. It was archaic to American eyes. The only comparable places I have seen prior to that day are Colonial American Forts, and British and Irish castles. The land felt unclaimed, but dutifully held watch over those that called Trondheim home. It had character all its own. It was not domineering or extravagant. It was simple and utilitarian, connected to the sea, and a staple of the land. The rain came down heavily as Einar and I explored the fort. I tried to wrap my head around the consciousness and energy that filled the fort in its most important moments, but that is only a spirit that can be gained through first-hand experience.

We walked down from the fort, through the park, and towards town. The dreary weather conjured maritime sensations; a calling for the sea. Was the calm of this city hidden in the climate? Complaints and excitement were quelled in the blanket of rain and clouds. The air was chilly, but not cold. The atmosphere lured souls from their armchairs, down the street, only to take shelter at the pub. There, the soul socialized, reconnected with the external human element that was kept so distant through the rain and chilly air. As we made our way from the top of the hill down to Nidelva, we passed homes. The day could have been two hundred years in the past, and I felt the homes would have appeared just the same. One yellow house bordered by small strips of grass and a white picket fence struck my eye. I felt a quant romance about the place as I walked past. In its presence, there felt no need for luxury or excess, only the necessity of home and heart. The people who lived there seemed to put feeling into the walls and roof that sheltered, yet connected and established them as members of the community.

On our way down to the pub, we passed a simple yet ingenious article of civil engineering; a bike lift. A small plate ascended a hill for an entire city block. Pay a few kroners and a metal triangle came out of a housing and propelled cyclist to the top of the steep block. It was the first in the world, and one of only a few on Earth. Einar was excited to show me. He's kind of a civil engineering geek, just like how I get a little too excited about rocks, soil, and water. Either way it made me think about small luxuries that could make tedious or strenuous tasks bearable for everyone. If small luxuries like this were more readily accommodating to simpler modes of labor and transportation, then those modes would become way more common, and as a result technology would take a serious twist focusing on simpler tools for simpler work.

    We finally reached Bakklandet, the historic district of Trondheim. It stretched along the Nidelva for a few blocks composed almost entirely of tall wooden buildings along the river. In old days, ships would come up the river from the fjord with goods, and cranes hanging from the roof trusses of these buildings would unload whatever the ships may have brought in. The streets were paved in stones, an innovation pioneered by Carl Adolf Dahl. Dahl was the father of civil engineering in Norway, and one of Einar's heros. The paved streets made travel easier and kept mud out of the houses and the pubs. The streets and buildings delivered hints of the importance of the sea to this community. It was Trondheim's window to the world. The integrity of the structures had been held in tact, just as Tronders retained their connection to the water, and carried its spirit indoors to be shared with the people close to you who make life worth living. The camaraderie with the sea, the food, and the fare could be felt in Bakklandet

Skydsstation, the first pub Einar and I stopped at. The building was a few hundred years old, revealing its age with the tilt of its walls as its foundation crept downhill with the soil overtime. The doorways were small, built for people a little smaller in stature than the modern man. Two tables sat in the first room, no more than 100 or 200 square feet in area.

At the back of the first room, a counter held the cash register and a few beer taps. Behind it were shelves of liquor bottles and a refrigerator filled with bottles of beer. Dahl's was on tap, a Trondheim mainstay. Einar suggested I try it, so I ordered up a pint of Dahl's and a double shot of cheap scotch. We walked through another doorway to the side of the counter, and into another small dining room. This one was slightly larger. The walls still slanted with the creep of the hillside, but were decorated with traditional, Norsk tapestries. On them, circles surrounded intersecting strips of earthy tones of almost every color. Some tapestries sported lines of arrows in similar chroma. We sat at our table in the cozy pub and talked about the cheer that a pint of beer brings on a Sunday evening. The soul decompresses in and airy harmonic hum. It renders itself in time and humanity. We were sitting next to a group of middle-aged people enjoying a late dinner. One man joked that his friend should see America before Donald Trump gets ahold of it an ruins the place. I laughed to myself in pondering his words.

The spirit of the place and the people was beginning to spill over, even though my friend and I were in a different frame of mind than our company. Consciousness varies most drastically over small areas. In the local sense, consciousness is mostly a matter of time instead of space. When time is shared, consciousness has a local harmony. Over greater areas, consciousness becomes more unified. There, principles of humanity are found. I took a sip of my Dahl's. The maltiness was medium to light. It laid somewhere between Yuengling and Miller. The hoppiness was super mellow, just enough to almost detect a bitter flavor somewhere in the brew. The flavor suited the moment well, a gentle spirit of Bakklandet. Once I primed my palate with beer, I began to work on my scotch. The peatiness, the smokiness of the liquor was light, almost undetectable, but as I sipped my scotch and Dahl's, the two coalesced into satisfactory harmony. The flavors were just enough to propel the conversation between Einar and I into the next waiting moment. Brassieres and underwear hung on a clothesline in the courtyard behind the building. Einar snapped a picture, we laughed, and returned to our drinks. There was no sense of urgency in the moment. We just enjoyed our drinks in the old building. I was comforted with a warm, cozy place with the ability to comfort the rambler as well as the aristocrat. The rooms were small, but what they delivered in character could not be measured. The days of ole were connecting with the here and now. The aura of Norway's heritage was held in place during that ethereal moment when Einar and I matched our beers with the family next to us eating fish and vegetables. The mystic song of the sea rolled in with harmony that dampened any static crush that attempted to develop. The saltiness and tight wooden walls held steadfast. That decompressing hum filled my spirit.

After a round or two we moved on. The evening was getting late, but the sun was still high in the sky, peeking out from behind the passing clouds. Einar and I walked from Bakklandet Skydsstation down to Nidelva. A walkway bordered the river. We meandered along the bank, and made our way across some rocks out onto the water. "What kind of rock is this?" I asked Einar. He had no answer to my question. As I examined the dark color, and fine texture, my first thought was limestone, but this boulder was to smooth, and too round to be limestone. "This is basalt!" I exclaimed to my friend. He admitted that he didn't know, but I had enough evidence to prove to myself what the rock was. I was excited. The igneous rock was the make-up of all the bedrock in the area. Basalt lined the coast of the fjord. It extended up to the mountains we would hike later in the week, and exposed me to the sheltered environment I lived in. In the Allegheny Mountains, and Laurel Highlands, most of the bedrock is sedimentary; sandstone, limestone, and shale. Breaking the bounds of local geography and local geology exposes one to an environment that is totally alien, and new. Dark and smooth, the basalt cast a shade of darkness on Tronheim. Everything seemed to vibrate with a tone of obscurity. Trondheim was a good place occupied with good people, but it had a hue of mystery in its spirit. Everything about it left you asking 'Why' and 'Where from?' We left the basalt rock shores of Nidelva, and returned to the streets of Bakklandet.

I asked Einar where would be a good place to get a cup of coffee on Monday. He said he'd show me, but that got interrupted, and canceled. Instead we found a book-bar. Strange, I thought, but we walked in. The woodwork was old and seasoned. The tables were small and the lighting was dim. It was after nine o'clock, but most of the light produced in the room came in through the windows. The bar had a clean, yet pungent aura about it. The walls were laced with traditional Norwegian design, and the summer Sunday evening feel flowed throughout the bar. I was beginning to believe that that wavelength was continuous throughout the city instead of existing discretely from place to place.

As we walked in, Einar recognized one of his friends immediately. The man was slender with a Mediterranean look. Einar greeted his Kurdish friend with a warm embrace, and we walked to the basement. A small stairway led to a narrow hallway. The passage to the basement was aged, and had character. I felt cryptic in that moment. We reached the gathering room, and a microphone and speakers were in place to satisfy open-mic night. Books and bookshelves lined the walls, filled with old hardbacks with lettering of gold foil. The books did not feel out of place, although I, nor anyone else was indulging in literature. We sat down at one of two tables that were not occupied, and took our jackets off. I walked twelve feet, across the room, and to the bar. Dahl's was on tap, and I thought I would continue in the direction I was already headed. So, I ordered up some more Dahl's and a shot of Jameson. Henar (pronounced Hoonor), Einar, and I sat at our table near the window waiting for the host to take stage and speak into the microphone. There was a warmth about the place. With its low ceiling, and tight tables, a somber, reserved love connected everyone in the basement. Some conversations were in Norsk, some in English. Words glided gently across the lips and into the ears, warming the heart with their vibrations.

    Around ten o'clock, a man took the stage. He made no introduction, just started singing and playing guitar. His voice was warm with depth and rasp. He was pulling energy from somewhere down low in his being. The guitar riffs were bluesy and jazzy. Perfect folk-playing. The music took me back in time to a day I have not live, a time when there was more mystery in living. He sang mostly in Norsk, weaving in a verse or two in English. I was feeling the music. I tapped my foot, and slapped my knee, wishing I had my bass guitar with me. Energy grew, filling the soul of every person in the bar. It hit perfectly, consciousness wrapped around the rhythm, synchronizing all of us in time. Unified, we shared the moment.

The host (who also happened to be the owner of the bar) played one more song, and opened the stage for others to play. First to walk up to the mic was a black Brazilian boy, probably about 18 years old, and his female Norwegian complement. The young man played guitar and the girl sang. The feeling was consistent with the music that preceded the two. The lyrics were English, and the riffs had a dark, jazzy feel. "Breathing underwater – Breathing water in..." The duet had the house rockin'. There wasn't one person sitting still. Everyone was tapping their feet, and swaying in their chairs. The ovation the two received when they finished made them smile, and blush. They did it! I could only imagine the sensation they felt while they were performing. They produced something that everyone accepted and wholly enjoyed. The crowd was connected with, and captivated by the music. That's the whole objective of performing live music; getting the crowd to feel what you feel inside while you're playing. That moment when everyone hollers with applause is the punctuation that you know you made them feel alive. Your efforts hit the mark. That's the thrill of performing: knowing that you struck a nerve in souls of spectators. And when the music is an original creation the gratitude is that much more fulfilling. The audience isn't the only one(s) feeling alive.

Music is an extension of energy and consciousness. You take something within, and make it external through vibrations. It's a personal concept of the spirit, in an audible sense. The tones that breath through life. Finding particular wavelengths and frequencies, and recurrence intervals for those frequencies is where the challenge of inspiration and provocation through music lies. After the first duet finished performing, another duet took the stage, a Caribbean man and some hippy chic. Once again, she sang and he played guitar. Their music was a little more delicate. It made you relaxed. It was capable of bringing peace to a tense mind.

The music wrapped up shortly after 11:00PM. With a few drinks in bellies, and half a jag in the brain, we left the bar and made our way out of Bakklandet. Sunlight was still in the air when we walked out of the bar. Einar led me along Nidelva towards Solsiden (Sunnyside). Along the way I felt peace, and clarity in my soul. It could have been the river, or the sea, or the midnight sun. Most likely though, it was the spirit that those things cultivated within the people who called Trondheim home. That spirit had been spilling over to me the whole evening. Clean air with hints of salt were filling my nose as we walked. The Nidelva was dark and placid. Eventually we left the old buildings, and stone-paved roads behind. We arrived in Solsiden. It laid at the mouth of the river, where the river met the fjord. Red-brick buildings stood against red-brick buildings. Most of which were high-end restaurants with outdoor dining areas. It was close to midnight on a Sunday, so the restaurants were closed, but it was still light out. One of the places was an Italian restaurant Einar liked to go to for pizza, Una. After catching a glimpse of Solsiden, we headed south up the long hill back to Einar's apartment. It was still light out when I fell asleep on his couch Sunday night.

Day 3:

I first opened my eyes around 9:30 AM. The weather was clear and bright, but I wanted to catch up on sleep since I had the chance. It was nearly 11:00 by the time I made it to my feet. I got a shower, dressed, then tried to organize my things, separating clean clothes from dirty, and gathering toiletries and things of the like. Shortly before noon, I walked out the door of Einar's apartment. He left for work around 8:30 that morning, and left me with a key to the place. Before exploring the city without the guidance of my friend, I wanted to catch up on my travel log, preferably with the assistance of a cup of coffee. After putting a little distance between Einar's apartment and myself, I began inspecting the streets, sidewalks, and houses as I headed southwest towards Kristiansten Fort. I vaguely remember its whereabouts from the day before. As I began the trek through the Norwegian town, weeds poked through the patches of dirt that laid about the concrete. Building design was different from places I had been before. Every place on Earth has its own unique architecture. These are the faces of neighborhoods and communities. Geographic aspect filters through to the work of the mind and the hands. Inspiration lies within the natural environment. Practice is derived through experience, as we gain an understanding of what works and what doesn't. It was Monday so most people were at work, but I could imagine people filling the houses, or roaming the streets within an inner joy of the simple pleasures living in such a place could derive. There were numerous people on the sidewalks, but few cars passed down the streets. The sun was bright on the lawns and the buildings, and everything looked cared for in necessary proportion.

Eventually I made it to Kristiansten Fort. The café was closed, but I felt like there was something there that I did not see yesterday. I walked down a footpath, and through a tunnel and found myself perched high above Trondheim. I sat there at a picnic table. Nearby, a man was meditating, and a woman was sunbathing. It was the perfect place to sit down and recollect what I had experienced since I arrived in Norway. I though about the way the place made me feel. The sun was shining, and there was a pleasant breeze blowing. The air temperature was in the low 70's. I opened my travel log, and ran my fingers across the heavy, coarse-textured paper, and looked out before me as I chewed over everything between Saturday morning, and that moment at Kristiansten Fort.

My eyes saw grass, meeting fortress wall, meeting sky. I put pen to paper and thought about the airport, Oslo Sentrum in the sleepy morning hours, the beer, the futbol, the night, the flight, and the rainy welcoming to Trondheim. The sensations the spirit of Trondheim had to deliver on Sunday evening in the last days of spring were magical. Mid-day Monday delivered a slightly different feel than Sunday evening. The clarity was there, but the somber isolation of the rain dissolved, and a fluent continuity began to develop. The city was breathing, and beating, but it did not lurch and stagger with intimidation. Even to me, an alien, Trondheim welcomed me. I sat high above the city jotting down my account of Norway, and the significance of each moment onto paper with my blue ink pen. The feeling was ethereal. The sun, the clear skies, and the breeze coaxed my account and perception of reality. The moment cleared my mind. It was a spiritual moment as I sat there at the fort. I felt like an individual, a unique, discrete being, but at the same time I felt unified with the world I was living in. I would jot down a few sentences then ponder my thoughts. My eyes slowly glanced across the fort to the man mediating, then out to the sky. The woman against the low fortress wall was closest to me. I looked back and forth between the two of them and back to my notebook. I sat there and wrote with direction, and clarity for nearly two hours. Then, when the grounds-crew approached our area with lawn mowers, the three of us left within moments of each other. Us three were connecting with our environment. The woman was primarily interested in feeling the energy, sunlight. Electro-magnetic in sorts. Us men tried to make sense of the energy and consciousness on our own terms, connecting the dots on a similar wavelength. I was in this new land, with a new heritage, a new tradition, and a new spirit. As the three of us left, tourists continued to walk about where we sat, and take pictures, attempting to capture the moment, and make a connection with themselves, and that particular time in space. There was a definite continuity, mostly between me, the mediating man, and the sunbathing woman, but everyone there shared an atmosphere. Yet each of our perspectives were finite within the ego. I had my pen and felt the aura and consciousness of the other two. I felt wrapped up in a glimpse of time where three souls converged, ever so slightly.

I left Kristiansten Fort on the foot-paths cutting through the park just below. The grassy park stretched across the gentle hilltop slope. Then, went down the side of the hill through a wooded lot. The crowd of trees separated a few neighborhoods, and as I strolled through I felt isolated within a natural ethos of the historic Scandinavian city. There was a neighborhood I saw the day before, that I wanted to take a photograph, but missed my opportunity. It was the quaint yellow, Norwegian house, with a meek lawn, and white-picket fence. I passed through a patch of woods, and found myself amongst houses, and apartments. I couldn't tell which direction the house or neighborhood was from my current location. I gave up. I thought "I'll just get a beer in Bakklandet, and continue writing." So, that's what I did.

I moseyed downhill until I found myself on the stone-paved streets of Bakklandet. I was surprised by the crowd that filled the neighborhood on a Monday afternoon. Plenty of people were on the patios eating, drinking beer, drinking coffee, and there were plenty of people on bicycles roaming the streets. I guess a city is never truly vacant of leisure. There are always a few people who can afford to treat themselves to a morning, a day, an afternoon in effort to unwind the knots from the soul, and re-wind it in a bit more harmonious pattern, even through the week in daylight hours. Some of those doing the un-winding and re-winding were like me, tourists. Some spoke Norsk in Tronder dialect. Some simply spoke some Germanic tongue (German, English, Swedish, Norsk, Danish) and that felt in place in Bakklandet.

I made my way to Bakklandet Skydsstation, the tiny pub we stopped at Sunday, I and ordered up a pint of Guinness. I took my glass and walked to the sidewalk in front of the restaurant. I took a seat in a folding chair, and placed my beer and notebook down on the wobbly table. I took a few long pulls on my cool coffee stout, then glanced over what I had written and where I had let off. One more long pull on the Guinness, and my pen printed the language that described the personal significance I felt as I interacted with a foreign environment. I tried print as much as I could, but I wasn't making much progress. After all, the record would be typed. I think the important part was that I began trying to characterize, and personify what I saw of Norway. I'm glad I put as much thought and feeling as I did into my words in the beginning. The beginning was my first impression, and they say first impressions are the strongest. Once I realized the week would pass without the opportunity to really write the whole thing out, I gave up on capturing the spirit of this land, and just wrote the sequence of events in chronological order. I sat there, drank my Guinness, and logged the trip. The beer tasted especially delicious on that warm, Trondheim afternoon. I contemplated coffee, but I thought coffee stout might be a better fit, at least for now, then move on to the java after I get half a jag about the brain. I quickly finished my beer, maybe too quickly. I wasn't ready to leave, but I wasn't ready for another beer. The day was bright and warm. Beers in those moments are extra satisfying. No rush to get drunk while leisurely at work puts the pint down the gullet ever so dutifully. With beer gone, I slowly pulled myself out of the chair, leaving the glass behind, and moseyed down the street.

It was about 1:30 in the afternoon when I arrived at Folk&Fe, a coffee shop. I walked in, and a barista addressed me. I can't remember if his first words were in English or Norsk. I told him I wasn't ready to order yet, and let a pair of young ladies in front of me. I stood on the earth-toned tile floors and glanced over the black, slate counter tops. The baked goods in glass decanters caught my eye. I went back to reviewing the list of coffees on the board overhead, behind the counter. "Whats a Tors Hammer?" I asked the male barista. He said it was coffee with espresso. I ordered a small cup then the barista asked "Would you like some tarta?" Finally, the Swedish tutorials paid off! I declined the offer for pastries, and took a seat at a counter looking out onto the old-world street. Continuing in my journal, I made it as far as my account of Helena at the coffee shop in Oslo two days prior. Along the way, my Tors Hammer give me a little kick. The strong, slightly bitter brew tasted nice on my palate. The hazy comfort of the Guinness a few moments earlier was driven away with caffeine. I hadn't eaten anything yet, and the shrimp rolls in the decanters looked tasty, but I figured I'd wait it out until Einar got off work, then we could go for dinner together. The café was quiet. It smelled delicious, and wasn't all that different than something you would see in a trendy part of any nice city in America; slate, earthy tones of tile, and wood. The scents, sights and tastes delivered an atmosphere of class and sophistication that spoke in relaxing notes. The idea was to brush the surface of what Bakklandet had to offer, and the stroke of Folk&Fe brewed a nice 20 minutes.

3:00 PM arrived as I sat on a bench at a corner in Bakklandet. The sun was bright and warm, piercing through the cotton of my white, long-sleeved shirt. Across the street laid a patio where people ate and drank. The people were plentiful, and I could see feeling. Happy and excited expressions were on their faces. Pain and depression seemed removed from Trondheim. That's an idea I didn't give much consideration while I was there. I just tried to immerse myself into the culture with a little guidance from my friends. Norway is supposed to be one of the happiest countries on Earth. Without looking for it, I found that treasure. Our most prized discoveries are often those we were not searching for. They are ones that appear before us without warning. They are things we often did not know existed. That would be a good reason they are not sought after with planning and forecast. These things are intrinsic and intangible, and make each place on Earth special and unique. The happiness from the patio nearby where people were eating and drinking was spilling over. We blended, them and myself, or possibly more accurately I assimilated to their comfort and relaxation.

Soon, Einar met me there, arriving directly from work. We greeted each other with smiles. We crossed to the north side of the Nidelva, and walked west along the shore. A park stretched nearly a kilometer along the shore. The long strip of grass was occupied with people throwing Frisbees and kicking soccer balls. There were lots of people, but they did not have to crowd each other out. The bright skies, and warm air attracted a few hundred people to the park to take in the final days of spring. The park felt welcoming. There was nothing intimidating about it. There was no persona of ego that I could detect. Trondheim felt like a whole-heartedly happy place. Einar and I walked side-by-side, westward, enjoying Monday afternoon within the jovial, sincere atmosphere. He wanted to take me to the Dome-Church (Nidaros Cathedral). He told me stories about the place. Once an angel was refaced to look like Bob Dylan, and as local legend goes, if construction of the church is ever complete, the city will fall. We turned away from the park and walked back an alley, and got harassed by a seagull as we approached its chick. Along the way, we passed the backside of small buildings; bars, restaurants, cafes. None of them felt upscale, high-class, or grossly dignified. There was no status to be met, just an expectation of respect. We made it past the seagull and the chick, and walked out of the mouth of the Alley.

Einar hoped to get a bite to eat at one of the cafés, but it was closed until a later hour, so we continued on.

In a short while we found ourselves standing at the edge of a big stone patio, opposite the cathedral with its stone sculptures and oxidized, copper domes. It was not as grand as St. Peters Cathedral in London, or St. Patrick's Cathedral in Dublin. But there was a spirit about it, an affirmation in the consciousness that removed people from archaic gods, and placed the soul and the spirit in the hands of Christ. The Gothic architecture bridged the gap between Viking, and Christian religions. I felt like I was witnessing a limbo between what was, and what came to be. We passed under a circular stained glass mural depicting Armageddon, stretching 20 meters in diameter as we entered the Cathedral. A long choir hall extended in one direction, and was intersected with another vein of hallway. Two or three organs sat in the cathedral. Both were handcrafted, one of which was of the best design in the world, with only two others like it in existence. The stained glass pictures near the ceiling depicted Old Testament Stories on one side of the Cathedral, and New Testament stories on the other side, both in chronological order, reading right to left. Despite all the art and architecture of the building, and the compelling story of St. Olaf, patron saint and once king of Norway, the cathedral felt empty. It felt like little more than a stone building.

I'm not sure what the ethos of the spirit was. I'm not sure I could identify what was sustaining the soul. It was too foreign. I tried to reach out and connect with the energy and consciousness that the cathedral was supposed to harbor and represent, but I felt nothing. The cathedral was an icon of religion, not a home of the Holy Spirit. Such divinity only dwells where it is accepted, and communicated with, but as I stood in Nidaros Cathedral, the Holy Spirit felt dead. The cathedral was little more than a tourist attraction in modern times with occasional ceremonies taking place within the walls. Most of Norway is atheist or agnostic. The lack of divine energy and consciousness that I searched for in Nidaros Cathedral was evidence that the Holy Spirit reacts to the people, places, and things, that request it. It wastes nothing on trying to fill vacuous space in an attempt to prove itself to blind eyes. Spirit is something that exists only for those searching for it. It does not exist in vain satisfaction of itself. No, that day I did not feel the Holy Spirit in that place, but the tour guide told stories of miracles happening around the tomb of St. Olaf, and a Holy spring running near his tomb. At one time Nidaros Cathedral was an icon of what the people of Trondheim believed in. It was a symbol, a physical manifestation of the intangible things that existed in humanity, and our realm of consciousness. At the height of Christianity in Norway, people would travel great distances to see the tomb, and drink the water from the spring. So there was a day when the Holy Spirit dwelt within Nidaros Cathedral, but that Monday, as evening approached, the spiritual days of Nidaros Cathedral felt as though they laid far in the past.

    We left the cathedral, and I was pleased to have seen the place. The gothic architecture was the first I've ever seen in person. It made me consider the immortal and other-worldly beings. It spoke whispers of the great Norwegian heritage, Viking heritage, as those were the origins of St. Olaf. Anyway, we left, and I took its impressions with me. Einar and I were in search of food and beer. The hour was approaching 8:00 pm, and the skies were still bright. The sun was nowhere close to the horizon, and we stomped around the streets of the Market District of Trondheim looking at architecture and engineering. It was an urban landscape. Buildings were not crowded, nor one on top of the other. The structure of the city was as relaxed as its people... for the most part. Einar showed me a house built for a wealthy woman. He explained that empty space laid between the walls so that the spacing of the windows and outward appearance was grander than it really was. It was superficial luxury in an attempt to appear wealthier than others, the poor and working class in particular. The house was made of wood, and if Einar didn't explain the story behind it, I would have taken it for a boarding house or something of the like, but in fact, it was a status symbol. There was a beautiful gated garden just to the side of this house. Tall, mature trees shaded the spit of grass and walkways. Benches comfortably nestled themselves into the garden providing a place to sit and privately embrace the city in all of its good, bad, ugly, and beautiful faces. We continued about, and I had a hard time keeping track of our direction, and relative location. We wandered away from the central market district, passing through a shopping mall, and Einar began delivering me options for places to eat. One of which was an Italian restaurant, Fratti. I was hoping for traditional Norwegian cuisine, but Einar said there was plenty of seafood on the menu at Fratti, and that sounded pretty good.

Eventually we arrived. As we walked in, we hoped for a seat on the patio, but it all looked occupied. Just inside the door, we were meet by a hostess who Einar knew. He seemed to know a lot of people in town. They spoke in Norsk for a minute then English. Einar convinced the hostess to clear a table outside, and she seated us. Fratti reminded me of the high-end dining establishments in Solsiden. The architecture must have been the mode for modern Norwegian dining; large, open-spaced dining inside, with the island-bar in the center. The lighting inside was dim, and all of the structure was formed from wood. Outside was a combination of wood, iron, and synthetic furs. It screamed Scandinavian luxury in classic tones. Soon a waiter came to our table. When asked what I'd have, I ordered a Norwegian Blonde Ale, and looked over the English version of the menu. I don't recall what Einar ordered to drink, but he got an appetizer of Blue-shells, mussels, which he shared with me. The flavor of the mussels were briny, but not too fishy. The texture was visceral, but not chewy. I worked at the mussels slowly and drank my beer as I waited for my entre. Before long my plate of Monkfish, mashed potatoes, and steamed vegetables was delivered. The plump white fillets were browned lightly in butter. The texture was delicate, and as I took my first bite, it reminded me of lobster. The fishiness of the meat was almost non-existent. The impulses from my taste buds sent pleasure surging throughout my body. I gobbled down most of the first fillet with delight, and sincere satisfaction, then worked on the mashed-potatoes. The spuds had hints of cheese and garlic. The consistency was perfect, as if cooked by my own mother, and the vegies were al-dente. Einar ordered a pizza with prosciutto and rockets (arugula). I had a slice of his pie, and it was much better than the frozen pizza served up at many-a bar. The pizza did not send me off into bliss like my monkfish, but it was good. I finished my beer before I made my way through most of my meal, so I ordered another drink. A brown ale this time. Its taste was strong; a heavy maltiness that was outweighed by spicy hops. The Blonde Ale was a better compliment to my dish, as it didn't outweigh the flavor of the food. I enjoyed both beers, but there is always one on the menu that fits the food best.

  We finished our food and drinks, and waited for the waiter to return with our bills. I paid in credit card and forgot to add the tip when I punched the payment amount into the portable keypad. So, guilty as I felt, I waited for him to pass again and handed him a 100 Kroner note. He smiled as if he expected me to stiff him on a tip. With full bellies and all scores settled, Einar and I left Fratti in search of more beer. My friend suggested a brew pub. So, we took direction, making a slight detour so I could by snus at a grocery store, then closed the ground between ourselves and the craft-beer-garden. The hour was about 9:30 PM, but the sun was still high in the sky. There weren't many people at the brewpub, which makes sense considering the Monday evening hour. I ordered an imperial stout poured slow-tap style. Einar finished his first beer before I was even served mine. He joked about the wait. Way-too-slow-tapped. I just thirsted in slight regret of my decision, but the beer was delicious once it finally hit my palate. The density and viscosity of the black liquid tasted smoother than any other imperial stout I've ever had. It was bitter and smoky and delicious. After I finished my stout, Einar and I moved on. It wasn't quite yet 10:00 pm. We walked toward the marina, where the docks met the fjord. Along the way we passed the markets that sold fresh seafood and salmon. It was well after business hours, but standing before the tall whitewashed storefronts one could look in on the dining situation. We hoped to make time to shop there before I left. The whole street spoke tones of sea-fare. The omniscient cleanliness that the sea delivered was present by the store fronts, even after they closed for the day. The marina laid just on the opposite side of the street. Sailboats and motorboats both occupied the docks. All of which were big enough to handle some degree of rough water. Those boats were a far cry from the 16 foot john-boat I captained on the Ohio River. We worked our way through the marina, past the train station, and onward to Sky Bar.

When we walked into Sky Bar, it felt like some sort of corporate establishment. The floor was easily over 1,000 square feet. The industrial carpet gripped my boot-leather, but the uber-chic-post-modern furniture and décor mocked my brown, canvas pants, and Widespread Panic T-shirt. Einar led the way to the elevator, and hit the button for the 7th floor. We went up, and when we stepped out I was greeted with a room walled completely in glass. Brilliant sunlight shined across the fjord, and into Sky Bar conditioning keen eyes, and salty breath. I ordered a pint of Dahl's, and

Einar led the way out to the deck. A sets of tables and chairs coupled with burlap lounging pads lined the length of the 50 meter long perch. It was quarter after 10:00, and the sun was beginning to get low in the sky. "This is spectacular" I said as I looked out onto the fjord as it shimmered with sunlight. "This is what it's about. Traveling." Einar replied. We went on, back and forth, about finding that place, that moment that makes you reconsider everything you thought you knew about life. This was the high end, the positive end of the spectrum. Both of us hinted around about the other end, the low end, the bottom. It wasn't a philosophical pain we were ready to debate and consider. Instead, we enjoyed the pleasure at hand. It was surreal, yet it didn't meet my expectations. I was satisfied, surely, but there were other moments in life that were much more fulfilling. Maybe my trip to Norway wasn't about the highest of highs, or maximum fulfillment. No, it was just about an adjustment of perspective and recharging my batteries. Einar and I made a toast to 'The Good Life,' basked there for a few short moments, then moved on.

    The sun was low in the sky, and the buildings were casting shadows upon the streets. Twilight was setting in. It was close to 11:00 PM, but it still felt early

Back home, I was used to darkness fully embracing the air by 9:00 at night. The length of day made me feel tireless. The light was like an endless source of energy. As we put distance between ourselves and Sky Bar, we crossed back over the marina, and into the city. Our first stop was at a stone statue of two men. It was dedicated to all the men who went out to sea and never returned. It was a notion I never gave much consideration before that moment, but when I saw the statue and the commemoration, I thought about the countless families who lost loved ones, and never had closure or explanation. Sailors have been leaving the ports of Trondheim for centuries, and over the years the sea had to have claimed scores of lives. I tried to comprehend the mortality of a whole crew of men by the hands of a hungry ocean, but it was more than I could comprehend. Like most things, that is an instance that could only be grasped by living through it. We left the statue, and moved further into the city. We bopped down a wide alley with the detachment of the families of lost sailors in our mind, and came to another sculpture that transported the mind to the sea. The crude shape of a boat cast in stone sat at the head of a placid pool of water. Einar explained that it was another piece of art dedicated to the power of the sea. The simplicity of the sculpture, and the calm of the water brought a reverence over my mind, maybe the same reverence that comes over the soul in the moments after the sea claims one's life. We each had the other take a picture of ourselves sitting on the sculpture, then turned in the direction of Einar's apartment. We were on our way back, but there was a futbol game scheduled to be on television at the time, so we stopped at one more bar.

The bar was in Solsiden, at the bottom of Einar's hill. It was a European sports bar; high ceilings, lots of wood work, and the bar was in the center of the multi-roomed floor. It was getting late, and our minds were beginning to tire. You could hear it in our voices, but our conversation didn't lack in depth or participation. The subjects of self-respect, and facing adversity came up. Too often people stay quiet, in family matters, and in societal issues, when another body hacks and belittles them. People have their worth undermined by others and choose the comfort of familiarity over justice. They keep quiet simply to maintain the status-quo. Peace is something that is ever evolving, and involves proactive efforts to stabilize harmony. It is not something that magically appears out of passive temperaments. It has to be fought for, and in that fight, sacrifices must be made, and toes will be stepped on. Knowing what is right is the first step, and taking action to put those ideals in place is the necessary follow-up. When you fight for justice you will be faced with challenges, but in facing these challenges you will discover shit about yourself, good, bad, and ugly. Those who never have had to face adversity, are the ones I feel bad for. They never had these revelations of self-discovery. They go through life numb and blind, and when a weight shakes their concept of reality, they shatter. The futbol game was over, and after two rounds of beer a piece, we were ready to go home and turn in for the night.

Day 4:

I woke up early Tuesday. I had somewhere I wanted to be. The alarm clock rang out seven. The first train to Steinkjer (Stine-sher) left Trondheim at 8:10. Einar made a bowl of oatmeal for me, and I topped it with raisins and honey. I didn't have the gumption to shower and dress in time for the eight o'clock train, but there was to be another one an hour later. I was cleaned and dress by 8:35 and left the apartment. When I got to the train station, I was having trouble buying my ticket again. It seems language and customs aren't the only things that change in different lands. Computer systems have their assimilation as well. It was kind of Amtrak. Only kind of though. A bit more maintained. More up to date. I approached the woman at the help desk, and she got me a ticket. I walked out to platform #4 and within a few minutes the train arrived. The doors opened, and I stepped aboard. The train was clean, and slightly more luxurious than American city-trains. The boarding car was all hard surfaces with orange grab bars. I walked into the first coach car and was greeted by cotton, upholstery seats. I took a seat near the front, took off my bag and coat, and sat down. I had a ticket to Steinkjer.

That I knew. What I would find there was unknown. I wanted to see what a small Norwegian town had to offer. I come from a place where the population is small. The means of sustenance are natural. Life revolves around natural resources. In my mild research, Steinkjer seemed to hum along the same wavelengths. I wanted to meet people from Norway who lived lives in the same way I did in my Pennsylvania home. Or, at least I wanted to see how similar their lives were.

The train began rolling. The tracks followed the fjord as the water seemed to reach into the mainland endlessly. We passed homesteads, forests, and fields. The land cleared of forest got me thinking. Is the countryside of temperate western countries universally defined by fields and pastures? Maybe. Midwestern America, and Appalachia are a breath of hay and cornfields. Great Britain and Ireland are landscapes of ground cleared of their forests all the way to the sea. All that has not been cleared for agriculture is land that is too unruly to cultivate. The coast, cities, suburbs, and rugged mountains occupy the void of farmland I suppose. And, in Appalachia, natural succession reverts land once cleared for farming back to brushy thickets and forest. The food dwells there, berries and meat, things of that sort. Yes, this phenomenon is aesthetically displeasing, but a more visceral wonder is that of ecological health, wellness, and stability as we clear forest and cultivate crops. The crops feed society, but would the world be better had these lands been kept pristine. Hunter-gatherers competed to survive. Individuals, and communities who were incompetent in negotiating the Earth and all her bounty would be lost in history. Without the wisdom of the natural world, mechanics and all, we would have no insight of ourselves and what believe in, contributing nothing more than a fossil record. Through the activity of seeking the fruits of the Earth, people would develop closer relationships with creation, and the spirit that lives within it all. An understanding of who we are, and where we come from would become more apparent to the human race, throughout. But, most importantly a stronger sense of appreciation for all the natural wonders would develop within the individuals and communities that master survival of the fittest. These are the people who would rejoice in all the enchanting faces of nature. These are the people who, through great diligence and sacrifice, would feel whole in the light of the moon, as well as the shade of the trees. We would become a race of fluid beings as we feel the river that runs between the mountains. We would feel the pulse of the world, and live by the rhythm of the day, and the pace of the night. Greed might very well not exist, as the struggle to survive would prevent the jealousy of luxury. But humans would not be the only benefactor, as the species who survive on the coat-tails of the developments of man would be out-fought by those who are more fit to survive in a world that follows nothing more than geo-spatial succession. Field, and forest would exist in great expanses. Populations of plants and animals would exist in vast mosaics, every one wild. The loss of wilderness and exploration in the wilds is painful to see.

      The train progressed through the country side of west-central Norway, and my palate was tantalized with an exotic landscape. Despite the differences, it was not extremely different than where I call home. Forest reached down from the mountains to meet the minimal beaches of sand and silt. Saturated ground laid where the tide inundates at its highs, and leaves it barren upon its lows. Fields and pastures were evenly smattered across the landscape, as it mottled the contiguity of forest. Stands of conifers were mixed with a lesser population of hardwoods, and forbes. Species diversity was not very high. This was a specialized landscape. It was one that preferred persistence over production. It had to as the opportunity to create fuel from sunlight hit both extreme ends of the spectrum; 3 hours of light in the winter, and 3 hours of darkness in the summer. The temperature never went out of control despite the length of day. The high zenith angle, and low solar energy never scorched the landscape. The water from the coast worked to moderate temperature swings, insulating, delivering high latitude ocean temperatures to the coast stretching across the width of the country. And, in winter these waters offered more temperate weather. Ultimately, the sea provided moisture throughout the year. It was similar to what I'd expect to find in the northwest coast of America. Perfect habitat for trolls (they are supposed to bring good fortune, according to Norwegian folklore).

The train made its stops at the dozen or so stations between Trondheim and Steinkjer. Some stops had shelter, some had buildings, and some were little more than platforms for awaiting passengers. The train wasn't exactly crowded. The last morning train out of Trondheim carried a few business men, and a few backpackers. The locality where some of the passengers left made me curious as to what the attraction may have been for said location. Friends? Family? Business? Nature? I hadn't the slightest clue. Eventually we reached the end of the line, Steinkjer, the final stop. As the train rolled in to town, I tried to scout the layout of the city. Large commercial retailers laid to the north side of the tracks. I couldn't get a good view of what laid to the south. Without a map, I made a careful, calculated pass on the town. I walked west until I came to a bridge, then crossed the river and the tracks to the north side of town. As I moved back to the east, I was careful not to meander too much through the side streets until I had my bearings about me. I stopped in a gas station to get a drink, and moved past a shopping mall. I was on the hunt for food, beer, coffee, literature, maybe a boutique. I was having a rough go of it on the north side for a while, then as I continued east and passed the trainstation on the other side of the river, I came to a building complex. It was modest, and circular with big glass windows. There was a senior center, a gym, then I saw it, bibliotec (library)! I had a copy of River Class and a copy of The Way Down just for this occasion, in hopes it'd expand my range of readers. When I walked in, the place didn't feel like a library. It was too new, too clean. There were lively people sitting at a table near the entrance conversing in good humor. I walked up to the desk where a librarian stood behind a computer and I made her acquaintance. "Hello, I'm an American author, and I was wondering if you would be interested in putting a few of my books on your shelf?" The librarian was slightly flabbergasted. Her eyes got big, and her jaw nearly hit the floor. "What would the price be?" she asked. I told her I was only interested in reaching readers in other countries, and putting the books on the shelf would be payment enough. She sallied her supervisor, and he informed me there was an English section of the library. He would be pleased to stock my books. With the exchange completed, I jumped at the opportunity for local advice on the location of a drink. All that was open at that hour was Madame Brick's, a coffee shop, but in Norway, that meant a place to buy a decent beer as well. The librarians directions led me south, back across the river to the "Main Streets."

Madame Brick's sat a block or two off the main drag. Its whereabouts were modest. Small apartments and row-houses with Norwegian design lined the street. As I walked, I came across a store-front with big windows, and cream-colored paint. I saw tables through the window before my eyes caught glimpses of the sign overhead. I approached the door and looked up, Madame Brick's. With two goals accomplished I opened the door and walked in.

There was little artificial light, maybe a few lamps, the rest came in through the windows. The dark, elegant wood derived a comfortable, homely feel. Square, neat, rectangular. Two tables near the counter were fitted with company. I heard some English, and some Norsk course the airwaves. I met the counter, and shortly a cashier came to my service. "Do you have beer?" I asked him. He showed me the list, and I asked if he had any stouts. He explained two, one of which was bitter, and by his delivery I could tell he expected me to take the smoother of the two. "I'll take a bottle of the Norgne Imperial Stout." He pulsed with satisfaction, whether it was in his voice, or his face, I can't recall. He served me the liter, glassing half of it and leaving the rest in the bottle for me to take with to my table. I paid and walked over to a corner table against the window. I dropped my bag and my coat, and pulled out my travel log, picking up where I left off writing on the train. A couple in their early twenties sat in the booth two places

down from me, away from the window. They spoke in
English. I wrote and drank with the company of cloudy
skies just on the other side of the glass. The alcohol, and
décor provided good inspiration and energy for a written
account of my impression of this slightly foreign world.

Soon I finished my liter of Norgne Imperial
Stout in the din of Madame Brick's, and took a look at
the menu written on the chalkboard by the entrance.
"Smörgas," sandwiches. I carried the more important of
my effects with me to the cash register, asked for another
beer, and what kind of sandwiches he had. Salmon,
chicken salad, and roast beef was his answer. I asked for
salmon with aioli. I regained my seat, and sat there
drinking. The writing slowed as I began to get drunk,
and hungered for my sandwich. Before long, the man
who took my order served me a plate with a thin, pink
fillet of fish on a single piece of bread, topped with
garlic aioli. The fish was uncooked, and folded over two
or three times to fit on the bread. This is not what I plan
to dine on when I ordered. Instead, it was more. The
semi-smoked fillet of salmon had a more oily texture,
and pungent taste. It was better than sushi. Lox, I
believe it was. The open-faced sandwich minimized the
impact of the bread, and let the salmon and aioli shine

through. The aioli was the perfect complement for the meat. It was creamy, savory, and robust. The three ingredients complemented each other perfectly, delivering something I thought to be more Norwegian than any food I had had so far. I enjoyed every bite, feeling joy each time the food hit my palate. Before arriving in country, this salmon sandwich was something I had hoped to find when I dreamt and wondered what laid in my destination. I worked on my sandwich, and washed it down with swallows of beer.

When I had finished, I gathered my things, and walked out. I had a jag on from the beer, and floated in ecstasy as the flavors of fresh raw salmon, and garlic aioli lingered on my tongue. The high made the streets of Steinkjer soft, and fuzzy around the edges, destroying any definitive boundaries or archetypes. When I reached the end of the block, I turned to the left and made my way to the main drag. The traffic putted down the street, slowing to a halt every time a pedestrian readied to cross. I walked into an organic health store. There were tons of herbal remedies and organic hygiene products. Nothing tickled my fancy. I walked out and continued down the main drag. The face of the street was no different than any mid-sized, progressive, American city. Steinkjer reminded me of State College, PA.

I walked along with a fuzzy frame of mind, and passed a guitar shop. I didn't go in immediately. First I passed it, then doubled back, and went in. Nothing exotic popped out at me. The shop was somewhat common, maybe a bit more organized than the place in Johnstown I go to get my bass serviced. Guitar, guitar, then there it was, bass, and what a bass it was. The body was cherry wood with a satin finish. The clerk saw me eyeing it up, and I asked if I could play the stick. Without any explanation or sales pitch, he walked me over to the sound room with my four-stringed companion, plugged me in and shut the door. I noodled for a riff or two then, began picking the notes to my favorite, original riff. I gave him some feels. He had hoped I'd give him some dough. The action was medium to high as I played music that meandered somewhere between blues and jazz. It started off slow and melodic. Then I picked up the pace, transitioned into the chorus, and as I worked my way back to the verse I improvised, and substituted notes and adjusted the rhythm. I went on having my way with the axe for close to 15 minutes. Then when I walked out of the sound room, the store-owner wore a grin from ear to ear as he looked at me and the bass. We began talking. I told him how much I enjoyed playing it, then looked at the price tag. As I tried to do the math to convert Kroners to dollars, the man told me the story about this model of Warwick bass. Warwick found a palate of cherry wood in the stock room, just enough to make 75 guitars. What was produced were 75 medium-high action electric bass guitars that resonate vibrations through the humbuckers with a frequency that could get Les Claypool hot and bothered. I finally did the mental math, and determined the bass ran about $4,000 American. There was no way I could afford it. I asked about the amp, which was quite a piece of equipment itself. That was $900, still more than I could afford. With the simple pleasure of a decent jam running through my veins I returned to the streets.

There were some things artsy, and some things culinary that caught my attention, but I paid no visits. I worked my way back toward the train station, even though my train wasn't going to arrive for another hour and a half. Along the way I saw a store. I was a little puzzled as to what they sold so I went in. Lots of home décor is what I found. I bought a table runner with a

Scandinavian design in brown and black for my mother, a troll for my youngest nephew, a moose medallion for my oldest nephew, and two sets of earrings; one for my niece, and one for whatever girl may steal my heart.

My adventurous side was satisfied with what I discovered in Steinkjer. A café beer, a good jam, and a little shopping. My day trip felt complete and I headed back to the train station. As I sat in wait for the 3:15 train, I read more of Rolf Potts' "Vagabonding". The skies were dreary, and the air was damp. I sat on a bench under the awning, and let my cognition explore the thoughts the book had to offer. I began getting excited as my eyes passed over the words, and ideas formed in my mind. The possibility that I could go vagabonding, I could travel on the long term became more and more real to me as I read on. I've forgotten some of the lessons in making long term travel a reality, but what I can recall from that day on the platform was that when considering the goal, establish a deadline, and stick to it. Allowing the prize to constantly exist in the future is just another way of avoiding the sacrifices required to achieve your goals. When I decided to go to Norway, I dove in and committed myself before I could over think it. As the date became closer and closer to the present, I honestly dreaded the reality of my trip. But, when I was finally on my flight into Oslo, I was grinning ear to ear thinking, "I finally did it!" Between the flight, and boarding the train to Oslo Sentrum, I thought to myself, "Next Friday is on its way, day by day. Don't pass a single opportunity." From that point on, every second was passed just enjoying the moment. That's important. Don't miss an opportunity to step out of your comfort zone, whether it is at home or away on an adventure. That's when you grow as a person, when you step out of your comfort zone. The fabric of your reality is stressed, and when the weight is unloaded reality retains a little of weight's impression. Eventually, my train arrived and I got on. A light rain fell as we followed the fjord westward. Between the food, beer, and weather, I grew sleepy, and slept for about half an hour on the train.

    I awoke before we closed in on Trondheim. Brushy vegetation began to mesh with hardscapes, and we arrived at Trondheim station around 5:20 PM. Einar walked into the station just as I was approaching the front doors. I told him about my day, and when I got to the part about lunch I said "sma gos" instead of "smörgas." Apparently, I told him I had a small goose

for lunch. We laughed hard for a little while. We made
our way home. Solsiden was along the way, and I told
Einar I was hungry. He ran over the dining possibilities,
and when he mentioned a burger joint, Söt, the sound of
which caught my fancy. We walked in. The bar was
small, but there was a patio which had no open seats,
and a loft which was mostly vacant. As I took in the
atmosphere, I could imagine hipsters sitting in the din of
the bar, reading, café racers parked out front, and Franz
Ferdinand playing on the stereo. There was pop-art
plastered over the wooden walls. The menu and
advertising delivered a message filled by guilty
pleasures served up with a hint of counter-culture. I
looked over the burger choices and I ordered a
concoction with cheddar cheese, dill mayo, jalapenos,
and lettuce. I think I ordered a Guinness to drink. Einar
and I walked upstairs, and took a seat in a booth. The
lights were dim, and the booth was spacious. Eventually
our pager went off and my food was ready. Einar ate
before I met him at the train station, so he stuck to a
liquid diet. I walked down to the bar, grabbed my plate,
and returned to the booth. In the first bite I could taste
the dill mayo, I mean really taste it! It was strong but
not overpowering. Sharp and smooth. Dill is one of

those herbs that offers robust tastes and smells. As I grinded away on the burger, the jalapenos tickled my senses with their crisp, slightly astringent flavor. The cheddar cheese coupled with the grease from the burger, and the creamy mayo to create an emulsion of savoriness. The lettuce provided a little extra crunch, complementing the peppers, and in a few savage bites, my burger was gone. I knocked back my beer to wash it all down. We were at the joint for about 45 minutes. It felt like three clips of time. Ordering, waiting, and eating. It was the coolest meal I've had. It was the modern spirit of solsiden. A little dark, a little delicious.

Before making it all the way back to his apartment, we stopped at the grocery store. He never kept more than three or four days' supply of food, so he found himself planning meals and visiting the grocery store a few times a week. He asked me what I'd like for dinner tomorrow, and we talked about Indian food, chicken prepared in some fashion. As we bought the ingredients for Indian style chicken, we ran in to a few people Einar knew. We talked and shopped, purchasing a kit with yogurt sauce, chutney, and a paprika based spice to cook the chicken in. I purchased a six-pack of

Nordland Pils, then we went back to the apartment with all the fixins for the next day's supper.

Once back at the apartment, we lounged about for a while. The skies were clearing, but still a little grey. It was the summer solstice; the day I had come for. Unfortunately, we weren't far enough north to have 24 hours of daylight, but Einar was going to help me make the most of the evening. He wanted to show me a section of Trondheim called Svart Lamon, the punk-rocker section of town. When we hit the street I had already downed two of my Nordland Pils pounders, and was down to three cigarettes left in the pack. Einars daypack came along with us, full of beer. Once at street level we headed northeast. We made it to the edge of Einar's neighborhood, then the graffiti started. It was a big black wall, maybe the side of a building or something, but the crude artwork spray-painted on the wall was a big F-bomb in the face of "the man". This was the counter-culture. I was just beginning to see the mark they chose to make. That's just what Svart Lamon was: the mark of the counter culture. Every society has those constituents who live life by a means other than the mode, other than the cultural norm. They are the grisly underbelly of society. Everything that a government wants to keep hidden. Their fears. The counter-culture exploits it, and waves it in the face of anyone in sight. Without the counter culture, society would make no progress. They would go flat, get stale, and no one would ever bat an eye at the lack of effort for solving the problems. The world evolves. Harmony and change with the future is pretty much the focus. Believe in something good and follow it with complete faith. The counter-culture is the leg of society where corruption and dishonesty within the government breaks first-surface among the citizens. That is not to say that this sector of society is more morally sound than other sectors. No, just more sensitive to those flaws that exist in managed communities. Morals are not always the primary tools when keeping the peace.

Pal led me through a small park. Within it, there was an unofficial boundary where maintenance ceased. The grass was tall, and a look in the direction where we were headed hinted of a ghetto. We walked through the tall grass, came to a 10-foot tall concrete wall, and passed through a tunnel. Once on the other side of the wall, something felt real, visceral, gritty. This is where color developed. This is where texture happened. In the backstreets, in the communities that lived lives of free will apart from the almighty dollar, people exposed their inner thoughts, emotions, and energy into something external that could be felt by all five sense when you came in contact with it. There were no paved streets, only one-lane gravel roads. Trailers, campers, and RV's lined the lane, most of them looked as though their days of mobility were left far in the past. Old vans, and busses littered the lots of tall, un-mowed grass. Christmas lights and lawn-ornaments littered the neighborhood. It looked like Christmas on Mars.

As we made our way to the end of the lane, the end closest to civilization, we came upon a warehouse with windows busted out. Einar said, before the electricity to the building was cut-off, the place played home to punk-rock shows, and a skate-park existed inside at one time. As we continued on, the structure of the neighborhood became a little more of what you would expect to see on the outskirts of a city. No more RV's with overgrown yards, and pink flamingos in the lawn. No, just buildings that were standing the test of time, maybe built in the beginning of the modern era. Small apartment buildings, things that took up a quarter of the block or less, with painted, wooden exteriors. Candles were lit in the windows, and I could imagine incenses burning in the rooms. Strange, tacky figurines stood on some of the window sills. It was a Norwegian ghetto, without a doubt, but these places have more feeling than most places. Emotions get roused, words get heated, and some form of self-expression gets expelled. Maybe a bit too vulgar. Often the world can be a richer place because of it. We just need to know how to lay off and hope the punctuation and extent of the relax is close to perfect. We walked past a bar, and I lit up the last smoke in my pack. The windows were barred, and cheap neon signs lit them. A spectrum of colors spray painted the face of the bar, and I looked like the bouncer was talking to a boy who looked barely old enough to legally be drinking, but the serving-age for alcohol in Norway is 18 so, who knows.

We made our way out of Svart Lamon via fjord-side trail. The trail wound between the basalt cliffs and the briny water as the sun was getting low in the sky. The smell of the sea floated into the nose as we walked the gravel trail. Shellfish and saltwater could be smelled in the air. We walked for close to a kilometer, talking about God-knows-what before we made it to our destination. It was a little cove with a sunken ship where Einar liked to go scuba diving. On a bluff above the fjord sat a picnic table. We hiked up, and cracked open beers.

      The hour was close to 11:30 and the sun was still shining. I lifted my Nordland Pils to my lips, and tilted my head back. The air was chilly and the beer was warm but I was loving life. Few words could describe what I was feeling in those moments on that bluff. I was at peace with the world, and felt like I had an understanding of what delivered that peace. My friend sat across from me, and in his raspy, Norwegian accent, his words heightened the high. He talked about things that appealed to both of us, things that were intangible, and could only be understood through experience. I felt a connection with time, space, energy, and consciousness. I felt as though the world was at my fingertips, however finite or vast it may be. I did not see the midnight sun. No, it laid just below the horizon to the north, but at midnight, the light that shined over the mountain was beautiful, a kaleidoscope of orange, pink, blue, and white. Below the sky were mountains that were hidden in the mask of their own shadow. Below the mountains was the fjord, shimmering in the light of the Heavens. Heaven and Earth was painted by a master-artist, and I was seeing it for the first time. The magnetics of Earth seemed to shift and adjust the Electromagnetic energy shining down from the sun as it drew closer to the horizon. It hung near the round rock of Earth for hours. The light was magnificent. No picture could truly capture what I was seeing. I would have never known this had I not traveled there and felt it all within the reality of my mind and the reality of this beautiful Earth!

Day 5:

We made it home around 1:30 AM Wednesday, and Einar packed a bag for our hiking trip Wednesday afternoon; coffee, boots, a shirt to change into after work, and water. I slept in Wednesday morning. Our celebration of the solstice left me tired. I was supposed to meet Einar in Bakklandet at noon. I never made it until shortly after 12:30. My tardiness was the lesser of the two problems we faced Wednesday. On the way out the door, I set down Einar's bag and most of our water leaked out of the bladder, all over the elevator floor. I did a quick "Oh Shit!" and grabbed the bag. The whole thing got wet. I went into the grocery store along the way to grab an afternoon's ration of beer, it was tricky keeping the water-bladder from leaking any further. With a sixer of Nordland Pils pounders in my own bag I tromped down the hill to Bakklandet where Einar was waiting for me. I told him about the water loss, and took a quick look to inspect the problem. The lid wasn't screwed on square. Fortunately we had enough liquid to get us through the day.

We made our way westward across town, crossing Nidelva as it twisted and turned on its way out to the fjord. Up one side of a hill, through a neighborhood or two, then down the other side. The houses were more similar to American houses in that section of Trondheim. Small wooded yards and shaded sidewalks patterned the landscape. Eventually we were brought back to a crook of the fjord where a marina was nestled into the shore. Boats n'at. Further west were the "7 Tops," 7 mountain peaks, all connected by a network of trails. We were unsure how many we would do that day, but both of us were excited. I was excited to see some of Norway's montane wilderness, and it was doubly a therapeutic exercise for Einar as he led me through the forest, and retreated from the city. The weather was hot, or at least much warmer than it had been since I arrived in Norway. Temperatures were in the 80's, and clear, blue skies kept sweat on the brow, and dryness in the mouth.

One last city street then we would begin our ascent, 250 meters upward in about 3 kilometers across ground until we reached our first peak. The first few 100 meters across the ground were steep. The trail didn't wind to accommodate the hiker, or cyclist. It went straight up. It was grueling, and I had a sweat rolling after the first 100 feet vertical gain. The steep hillsides were lined with conifers and moss. Sunlight masked the trail between the shade of the trees. The occasional stick of hardwood popped up, and with it was usually underbrush. Dark blue flowers lined the trail, dotting its beauty into place. The shade from the trees cooled the air, and a light internal breeze blew about the forest. It was an ecosystem that hinted of spooky enchantment. The shadow of the timber was soft and mystical, enhanced in its enchantment by the muffled insulation of the moss. Quietly, the imagination roamed through the forest seeking trolls and fairies. Occasionally, the trickle of a creek carved away the soil, and exposed a groove of basalt as the water worked its way down the hillside. The air was not sticky, and coming from a humid climate, that was the factor I found most memorable.

We walked, and walked, and eventually we came to the first lookout. Boulders of basalt covered with moss and pine needles jutted away from the hillside, and stretched out into open air where a soul could stand, and feel the vastness of the world. Why does vast wilderness, vast oceans, vast coastlines, and high elevation offer so much peace to the psyche? Such places clear the mind so well! There are the seemingly limitless bounds of space that one could argue let the imagination run wild, but I believe it's more than that. The imagination fills in the gaps of the unseen and misunderstood. The vast world I'm speaking of is one that has few gaps or unseen corners. But, even when the imagination is given infinite freedom a human's cognition can become cluttered. The frame of mind I'm trying to explain is one that has no interruption, no distraction. It is a frame of mind where logic delivers clear insight to any question in the mind, and erases all peripheral clutter. In these vast expanses of undisturbed space, time seems to slow down. It takes longer for an object, even an object of thought, to traverse the horizon. The mind covers more territory over less time, but the expanded frame of reference creates the therapeutic illusion of life paced at a slower rate. *With time appearing to move more slowly, we are set up to inspect and critique our ideas with more depth and accuracy.* Lies and fallacies are stripped of their disguise, and discarded. We begin to move at natures pace, and we feel its rhythm. With its vibrations and frequencies, only the most natural wavelengths can be sustained, and those rhythms reconnect the mind with truth and virtue.

At that first lookout, a bench was built on the rocky perch beneath a pine tree. I filled my lungs with fresh air as I looked out onto the fjord and the city. The location offered a perspective of detachment from the civilized world. I was no longer one within the city. I was an observer of what humanity has constructed where the river met the fjord on that Norwegian coast. High above town we caught our breath, took a sip of water, snapped a photo, and continued on. Not much further down the trail was another lookout similar to the first. We stopped to take it all in, and I felt at peace. The calmness over my mind and soul remained as the body trudged along, uphill. This day was different. This was not a day spent collecting the stimulation of civilization. This was a day dedicated to the soul of a man, the souls of two men. Einar had his, and I had mine. Whatever value his captured was his. If he chose to share it with me, then he chose to share it with me. If not, then that's how things were meant to be. I shared glimpses of what I thought and how I felt when we took our short breaks, but I didn't press our time to be focused around philosophical lecture and debate. There was too much beauty to immerse one's self into.

As we gained elevation, the conifers thinned, and more hardwoods poked through. The chaos of dispersal became apparent. We were *not* covering enough ground to see ecological changes resultant of atmospheric changes. That kind of variation in landscape development results in greater geospatial scope. No, instead we were seeing a mosaic of plant life as a result of chance, and happenstance. I continued to sweat as we climbed uphill. Einar wanted to take a shortcut up a tractor path. It was steep, but in less than a kilometer we arrived at the first peak, Våttakammen. It was a craggy protrusion about as tall as it was round, maybe 150,000 cubic yards in volume. Barren rock was spotted with soil and tree growth. The crag lifted above the ground. No protection from the wind. The peak had little to offer in the way of cover from the elements. A young couple sat near the face facing the city. Einar and I sat back away for a few moments, and when the couple left we took their spot. I cracked open a beer and lit a wood-tipped cigarillo only to find out that drinking in public was frowned upon. That did not seem strange, but the fact that I brought beer along for the hike did. I'm sure the sight of a beer can breeds contemplation of how much of a degenerate these degenerates are, filthy white trash. It was a decision not all my own, but regardless of the circumstance I enjoyed the brew as we looked out over the fjord and the city of Trondheim. I felt accomplished. I felt like I did something with my day. Though this ecosystem was not *wildly* exotic, it was new, and I was seeing it for the first time. I was broadening my scope of experience in life, and through those new experiences I was rewarded with fresh thoughts and discoveries of the mind. I was moving towards a harmonious state, a state where mind, body, and spirit were all balanced through activity and exercise. Healthiness and happiness go hand in hand. The circulation of spiritual energy flows through the body, expels the bad, and resonates the good. It's a means of embracing the soul of one's reality. Air, water, and gravity ingest and percolated through the person. The expression remains within the integrity. In that way harmony is more easily sustained. Hiking has always had a way of doing that for me, and the "7 Tops" were no different.

After I drank 2 beers, Einar and I moved on, climbing towards the next peak, Geitfjillet. Washed out paths crawled up hill, over roots and boulders. The brown earth and grey roots were bordered with grassy vegetation The inclination was less steep than the route to the first peak, and it seemed to come in terraces. The soil became thin and sandy as we hit the first terrace, and seemed to wrap its hand around us. After a while, a thick, leafy forb covered the ground without an instance of vacancy. Green all around. The forest had its carpet. Conifers filled every structural layer of the forest, from the under-story, to the canopy. Bushy pines reached out, and occupied much of the understory. And, hemlocks and pines stretched up to the sky. We were in a cocoon of vegetation. The plants in that community were extroverts. They reached, touched, and communicated with each other. It was as though there was no competition for survival. It was as though there was an endless supply of nutrients, sunlight, and water no matter the position. Closed in with vegetation, I felt like a troll, myself, as we slowly ambled through the forest. I felt like a secret that could only be heard from a few yards away.

Upon the next terrace about a kilometer uphill the vegetation thinned. White pines spotted the swampy ground, and meadows of a white dandelion-type flower sprawled across the flats of the hill top. Fields of the feathery flower spread off into the distance. The clusters of white, hair-like petals swayed in the breeze, as they were held tightly into the sepal of the plant. We trudged over boulders, and bridges that crossed the swampy ground. We were on a hilltop meadow, and the ground was swampy. The climate was quite a preferable preference, nearly a temperate rainforest. The mind was focused on progress, and the scenery was comforting. It was calm and ethereal, a wee dank. Me and Einar were drafting for the lead without much comptetiveness. He knew where we were going, and I could see the line to the peak. Eventually we arrived at the second peak around 5:45 PM. There were more people at Geitfjillet than Våttakammen. The area was bigger. The expanse of the peak was approximately 50 acres. There were a few facets to it, bogs and rock piles. Although it was the summer solstice, the late afternoon hour at 64 degrees north latitutde, and 400 meters above sea level seemed more like a dismal October evening back home than the second day of summer. The only vegetation at the peak was nestled into the crooks between the peaking outcrops. The peaks themselves were bare rock. We started the day at sea level and ascended to over 1,400 feet above when we hit our second peak. We were beginning to feel worn, and pressed for time. So, we decided Geitfjillet would be the furthest we'd go. We stayed up there, and drank two beers a piece. I smoked another cigar as we looked down on the forest that laid west of Trondheim. As we looked out, I thought about the skew and outliers of the risk-reward proportionality. If the risk was injury or death, then in this case the thing with little risk had high rewards. The risk of discomfort from idle time may have been the price we paid. Experiencing those slightly exotic, specialized plant communities breathed a breath of fresh air, fresh thought, and fresh sensation into my mind and spirit. The energy spent on ascending those two peaks left the body feeling both used, and useful. There was a communion between soul and nature that day, and I felt like I fulfilled a particular hunger, a hunger that starved for something natural within a foreign land.

With cigars smoked, and beers drank, we began our descent. We hadn't gone hard enough on the way up to feel rubber-legged on the way down. I was thankful for that. Still, the trails were steep and rugged. They tested our strength and stamina, but delivered an intimate, harmonic secret. We were fortunate enough not to twist an ankle or fall into rocks on the way down, and when we met the end of the trail, we had to rove and hustle a bit to catch a bus-stop where we were ahead of schedule. We missed the bus at the first stop we came to from leaving the trail. At the second or third stop we visited we were finally ahead of the bus. Einar paid both our fares, and we took a seat. I don't recall the complete demographic of passengers, but I do remember a particularly pretty girl sitting just on the other side of aisle from me. She was maybe 18 or 19 with dark brown hair, a round face, and pouty lips. Her eyes were soft, limpid pools of white, brown, and black. They were delicate and forgiving, as though a man could rest a lifetime of pain within them, forgetting it all. Her height was average, but her legs were long. Her hips and posterior curved and popped beckoning a gentle contour. Most of these judgements were made when the bus reached Solsiden, and the girl departed from the bus with Einar and I. It made me wonder what I had been missing in the sense of female compassion and intimacy through the course of my trip. Much has been rumored about European romance, and Scandinavian beauty to the ears of dreamful Americans, but I didn't experience it too intimately. I felt like I was missing out. That first conversation with Helena in Oslo left me feeling at ease with the female point of view in Norway, but I never dove deeper than mere acquaintance. I never shared intimate moments with a single Norwegian woman. Not a regret, for a great deal of energy, consciousness, and spirit were perceived into a porous mind, body, and soul. A mere fraction was left to hypothesis and assumption as the time for intimate experience was sacrificed for nature, culture, transportation, cuisine, beer, theology, history, architecture, and the midnight sun. Much would have had to have been sacrificed in those means for me to make a proper effort in intimacy. Once you get started on that trip, it ruins the effect if you run out before fulfillment. Still, I was not sold short on romance. That coastal air at that latitude had plenty of romance, only lacking in intimacy. I'm glad I made the choices I did. From Solsiden, we walked up the southern hill of Trondheim to Einar's apartment.

Back to Einar's place, and he was doing the cooking that night. It would be Indian food that we had purchased the ingredients for on Tuesday. Chicken cooked in paprika and other spices with a yogurts sauce and chutney. We cooked and ate. The food was delicious. It was built out of flavors I had never tasted before, at least not in that arrangement. Spicey, sweet, and savory were rolled into one mélange, and filled the belly with comfort and sustenance. The side of naan bread added to the comfort meter. The buttery, garlic flavored baked good was like a punctuation mark of the meal, something that was also new to me.

    We showered and hit the streets for one more night within the Tronder conveyor of inflection. We were headed to an English pub near the market district for a futbol match. Tonight was between Italy and Ireland. Einar had a crew of Italian friends living in town. He expressed his allegiance and support to Italy. When he asked me who I would be rooting for (with indifference in his voice) I bashfully admitted that I would like to see Ireland win. He giggled at my answer, and dared me to jump on a table and celebrate should Ireland score a goal. I looked at him with bulging eyes, and asked him if he was nuts! Opposing a roomful of Italian soccer fans did not seem like a good idea! No, I accorded my conduct along the lines of self-preservation and related such ideals. Along the way the evening sun seemed strangely familiar, as if the sun and I were perceiving each other from a new angle, and for longer stretches of time. We had seen each other extensively over the past few days, and it shone down on my face as if to say "Hey bud, follow me." The warmth and the light at that hour excited curiosity and admiration. I was beginning to feel a connection with that place, and those people on a mild, enduring wavelength. I thirsted for the community, but I was not parched. We stomped down the hillside, through Solsiden, and into the market district. The pub sat on the corner. The building was large and white with a Victorian look to it, very English in appearance. We walked passed the man smoking a cigarette at the front door, and into the pub.

Inside was dark and dingy, but life clenched in the fists of the dozens of fans packed into the pub. It was buzzing on a high frequency, making the knuckles white, and the hair to stand on end. We walked through the first room, into the second, and headed to the stairs in the back corner. Everyone on the first floor was watching the Sweden-Belgium match. We ascended to the second story, and shuffled through a barroom of soccer fans packed shoulder to shoulder. The beer was flowing, the match was blaring over the stereo, but was still drowned out but the chatter of beer-drinking futbol fans. The rooms were loud. We walked into the last room in the building to about 2 dozen Italia fans and 3 or 4 Ireland fans. Einar greeted a man with celebration as we looked for a pair of empty chairs. We separated for a moment, and I made my way to the bar for a pint of Dahl's. With beer in hand I nudged through the crowd, spilling a little of my drink as I shuffled my feet, and cut between people. Back inside the room with the Italia game, Einar and I found some seats along the wall. The game was under way, and scoreless a few minutes before halftime. The bar was buzzing. Friends greeted each other, and conversation spiked with excitement frequently. A person had to yell to be heard. It was everything I imagined a futbol match in a European bar to be, and more. An American would think those preliminary matches were championship games by the size and fervor of the crowd. For as much excitement as there were around the games, there was just as much in the pleasure of the company within the bar. Before the second half, Einar spotted his Italian friends they were seated at the wall furthest from the projector-screen, the wall facing the street from which we entered. Einar led as the two of us squeezed between tables, chairs, and people. We got to the back of the room, and found a couple of places to rest our asses. All of the people we sat with were from Italy, living and working in Trondheim. I sat next to a man named Diego. We talked with interest to each other, mostly about work I think, shouting over the crowd, and straining to hear each other.

Diego was sincere. So many people I met that week were. In that foreign land, communication derived an image of one's self in the people one communicated with. I think that's what I was beginning to see. I'm sure the fact that Einar was friends with most of the people I talked had something to do with the sincerity of those people. Einar was a really good person, open minded, adventurous, intelligent, and empathetic. And, Norway has a reputation for warm-hearted folks. But, I think there is some truth in my assumption: you see yourself in the people you meet. You try to find some common ground to start from, and you build ideas from that point. Those ideas are ones you understand, and you explain them in a way you understand. The person you're communicating with listens and responds along those wavelengths, and as a result you see yourself in the spirit of someone else. That's one of the most beautiful things about life, the unity of the human spirit. There is variation in each one of us, as spirit fills us in slightly different ways, but as we interact, we find a common wavelength. We make connections between our lives and the lives of others, and we begin to imagine life in the other's shoes. We feel validated when we see ourselves in other people. We feel like our mode of living is one that follows the universal good and a path to success (or at the very least an *identification* of the path to failure). It gives us hope that that universal good would carry us through in any environment, community, or society.

Italy lost the match to Ireland 2-0. The bar calmed a little bit, and we hung out for a while. I talked to Diego some more, and Einar introduced me to a few other of his Italian friends. I was spent, and nearing the end of interest and productivity. As the fresh names and faces continued to appear, I made my best effort to store them in my memory, but it was a hopeless feat. I wouldn't say I was running on fumes. No, that state of energy and consciousness I like to reserve for a different state of spirit. Instead, I was plain out spent, palmed out, and 45 minutes of conversation left that apparent to anyone who looked me in the eye. Italian names and Mediterranean faces spoke to me in English. Einar carried on conversations with them in Italian. It sounded fluent, but he claims it as a third language, and one not mastered.

I learned a lot about my friend that week. Primarily, how high a standard he holds himself to. Einar was the face I identified the Norwegian culture to both before and after my trip. When he was a foreign exchange student at my high school in America, I thought him to be charismatic, silly, and open minded. Hanging out with Einar was always a good time. When I spent time in his homeland, he was no different. He was open-minded and always up for a good time, but I saw a diligence, and taste for life that existed in a different form from that within my friends at home. It wasn't drugs or a good drunk that drove adventure. Music and art were not at the fore-front of his aspect of foreign culture. Work was not a burden on his life, although he admitted to me that, like many people in western society, he measured his success with dollars, but made time for the important part of life, people. When he arranged our stay with Erik in Oslo I felt a warm welcome. When Einar made the arrangements for our journey to Trondheim I felt care and guidance. That first evening in Trondheim, I felt acquainted with all the wrinkles and dimples in the character of a city that dates back to the days of the Vikings. The pubs left me feeling engulfed in the energy and connected with the consciousness of the city, and the hundreds of people passing through. The Dome Church, the restaurants, the bars, the futbol games, the art, the architecture, the hills and mountains, and the Fjord, it all delivered a spiritual sensation served up by a friend, a friend who I had forgotten how much of myself I saw in him. He was the host I desired to be should I ever get another chance to show someone my home. And, Svart Lamon. Einar showed me the gritty underbelly of his home despite the lack of association he claimed with that neighborhood. That was my midnight sun. That may have been what I was unconsciously thirsting for when I thought of a foreign city that could trace me closer back to my home. It had all been embraced. Now I could feel my last few reps of Dahl's nearing the completion of another set.

Day 6:

I slept late into the morning Thursday. I crawled off the couch with a somber reckoning in my head. This was my last day in Trondheim. At 11:20 PM I would board the night train to Oslo Airport for my 10:00 AM flight Friday. I didn't know whether to cry or wind my watch. I putzed around the apartment a little before finding any direction. "Should I pack my things first, or get a shower?" After dilly-dallying with my bag and effects for about half an hour, I got in the shower. I let the water run through my hair, and I scrubbed my skin thoroughly. "This is the last time I will shower here," I thought. I turned off the water, and gathered my toiletries from the bathroom. I dried them all off and placed them neatly on the washing machine that sat next to the shower. Once dry, I began putting on clean clothes. I noticed I hadn't gone through everything I had brought. Two or three shirts and a pair of pants never saw the light of day during my stay. The long-sleeved, linen shirt, and my flannel-shirt proved useful during my trip. But, like any novice traveler, I over-packed. I separated clean clothes from dirty, and neatly began packing my bag. First clothes, then gifts and my cell-phone charger, then toiletries. I outfitted my day-pack with the bare necessities for the journey home, and packed that into my bag. My phone and wallet were all that remained. I looked at my watch and it was nearing 1:00. There was one place in town that I had not eaten at yet, and it was one of Einar's favorites, Una Pizzeria. I grabbed the key, and walked out of the apartment with my wallet and cell phone. The day was warm, maybe the warmest day all week. As I walked down the hill to Solsiden, the trip felt like it was already over. I felt like my adventure was finished. I was making assumptions.

    I got to the bottom of the hill where one of the main streets ran upriver towards Bakklandet, and I waited at the cross-walk for the signal to change. Cars were passing by with their usual quiet diligence as the warm sun shone bright down onto the city. The signal changed and I crossed the street. In that moment I felt like I had disappeared. I felt like I departed before I left. I walked past a few upscale restaurants in Solsiden before I came to Una. I walked up to the hostess and she began speaking to me in Norsk. I said a few words in English, and she switched languages without missing a beat. I asked to sit outside. She offered table options, and I chose one in the corner of the patio. I sat at the small, elegant, wooden table, and breezed through the beer selection. The Nogne Stout caught my eye. I ordered one, but was disappointed when the waitress returned without a beer, and only the information that they were all out of the black brew. Instead of ordering a different beer I opted for a glass of water. The waitress gave me some time to look over the menu. There were a handful of Italian dishes, but I came for pizza. There were about a dozen pizza recipes, and I narrowed my decision down to two or three before ultimately deciding on N'duja (on fire). The cheese I did not recognize, but the kicker was "Super hot sausage" in the description on the menu. I placed my order, and within about 20 minutes lunch was served. It was a 14 inch pie with an even layer of sauce topped with dollops of spicy, red sausage, and a creamy cheese. I overlooked the cheese situation when ordering. What I got was not what I was anticipating, but I didn't let that deter me from enjoying the meal. I spread the dollops of cheese and sausage over the pie, and began getting to work with the fork and knife. The first bite lived up to the name, N'duja. It was the spiciest sausage I ever had, a rich 50/50 mix of meat and peppery spices. Red, potent, and bitey. It kicked and punched at the palate, delivering strong heat and strong flavor. It was delicious. In an attempt to balance the heat with something else, the creamy cheese provided that balance of that 'something else'. I would have preferred a melted layer of mozzarella, but this was just one more experience that I will remember, authentic Italian pizza in Northern Europe. Creamy curds and whey aren't my preferred preference to complement dough, sauce, and sausage. I worked away at the pie for close to forty minutes.

With just a few bites left, I couldn't handle the heat or creaminess of the toppings any more. At the waitress's next pass, I asked for my check. I still had a few Kroners left so I paid in cash. With food in my belly, I wanted to grasp just one more connection with the people in Trondheim before I left. When I handed the waitress the money I ask "How do you say 'keep the change' in Norsk?" "Behold de ressen" was her reply. With a smile I handed the waitress a few Kroners and told her "Behold de ressen." She smiled, tickled by my interest in her native language, and my desire to connect with her on her terms. I wiped my face, and drank some water. Then I stood up and walked out. Before making it to the exit, I passed my waitress and overheard her giggling tales about me to another waitress, something in

Norwegian. Then, amidst her words I picked out "behold de ressen." Something was hot that I dropped, and spilled over to that pizza joint in Solsiden. I pounded the bulleted points. I saw Trondheim on a Tronder's terms. I did my best to speak the language by whatever that meant per situation. Using dialect to connect my ways and their ways produced warm results. Tipping a waitress in her native tongue was few degrees above warm though. The hours between my meal at Una, and Einar's return to the apartment after work, were spent on his balcony taking in the sun.

Eventually, Einar made it home, and we started cracking open beers. "Do you wanna cook tonight?" he asked me. A moose roast spent the day thawing, and I was looking forward to some moose for dinner. I had more experience cooking game than Einar, and he was curious what I could produce in the kitchen. I went to work. First, I sautéed some onions and mushrooms in butter, and butter-garlic, and cut the roast into steaks. With the veggies and fungus cooked-down, I squirted some Italian dressing into the pan and added the moose steaks. They started sizzling and the food smelled delicious. I added a few drops of soy-sauce to the meat and let them cook on medium heat until blood no longer rose to the surface of the steaks. When I turned the stove off, the meat was dark-pink through the middle two-thirds. I cooked some more frozen spinach, and served the meal. With bounty before us, I was ready to dig into our meal. As I raised my fork and knife, Einar asked if I was going to say a prayer? I was flattered by his question. It made me very happy to hear someone request my blessing over our food before we ate. I said grace over our last meal together, and we dug in. We quickly agreed that the food was everything we had hoped to be. Einar was pleased with my cooking, and I was elated to have the opportunity to cook a meal around *moose* steaks. Perfection! We washed the meal down with beer, and passed a few moments on his balcony while the sun was high in the sky.

    Einar had plans for the evening, and asked if I wanted to join him. There was a memorial dinner for a friend of his who had passed away in recent months. My situation was rather peculiar. I thought hard about it for a few moments. Here I was, a stranger in Norway, and I was invited to a memorial dinner for a friend of a friend. I decided to go, and hear about a person I never met. All I would have would be an idea of how this man was remembered by his friends. I would only meet the impressions this man left upon those close to him. There would be no greeting and handshake. No, only kind words and a delivery of spirit that captured this man's existence. We left the apartment around 7:30 and walked down the hill, through Solsiden, and into the market district.

The rendezvous was an English pub once again. This one had a bit more polished brass, cleanliness, and class than the place where we drank and watched futbol the night before, but with the classiness, the place we went to Thursday night lost an element of raw character that Wednesday's pub had. A bit more fitting for the occasion The place was nice, nice enough to take a girl to on date. Einar and I didn't see our company when we arrived. We stood near the entrance, and tried to stay out of the way, as we waited for a familiar face. Eventually, someone walked out of the back room and greeted Einar. We ordered a round of drinks, and followed the man back to our crowd, a crowd where I was a nameless guest. I was self-conscious. How should I answer that primary question? "How did you know Kris?" The truth is all I could say, "I didn't. I'm here with Einar" I wasn't sure how well that'd be accepted.

We walked into the backroom to about ten people seated around a long table. I shook a few hands, and exchanged names with a few people, and took a seat just trying to get a feel for the appropriate mannerism for the occasion. It could have gone without saying that loud and exciting was not the appropriate spirit. Should I be dynamic? Should I try too hard? No, somber and sympathetic with a sincere interest in what these people had to say about their friend was the only way to go. I would be quick to listen, and slow to speak. That evening was a lesson in humility. I tried to make no impression about myself to anyone I talked to. I was there to witness memories. I was there to share the spirit of a man, *a man I did not know*. When this became known to Kris's friends, no one condescended on me. They did not make me feel like a phony for coming to a stranger's memorial dinner. I just kept quiet, trying not to engage in conversation, just listening to what others had to say.

After about half an hour of conversations, a man spoke up. He had a broad frame, long, curly, black hair, and an English accent. We'll call him Ian, as that is the name that seems to hold in my memory. Ian started with the obligatory 'why we are all here,' then moved along by saying, one at a time, tell us what you remember about Kris. Ian told his own memories of an opinionated English IT guy. As the stories flowed, they painted an image of a man who flew by the seat of his pants, a man striving for adventure, even though he took his blows in his perseverance. Kris made his friend's question their concept of love, society, and politics. A person like that is important in any group of friends. Without questioning a belief, would you be able to sustain proofs of logic or experience? Scrupulous examination is the first step in resolving flaws of any belief. The night was rewarding, but bitter-sweet. Stories of Kris's wife and young child surfaced, and the energy and consciousness took a back seat to the flesh and blood that was part of Kris. Parts of us can be sustained after we are gone, but there will always be a void of influence as the future becomes the present, and loved ones can no longer hear your voice, or feel your embrace. Men brought themselves to tears, and voices quavered as they recalled time spent with Kris. The hour was approaching for my departure, so Einar and I said our good-byes, and made our way out. Along the way, I said to Ian, "I did not know Kris. I said it sounds like you lost a good friend, but in a way maybe you will always have him with you."

Ian thanked me for the words, and with a bit a sentience shared, I began to make my way back to the apartment to grab my bag, and catch my train.

On the way back to the apartment I was pestering Einar about time constraints, and trying to push the pace. We had what seemed like a lot of ground to cover, roughly a mile to the apartment to grab my bag, then over half a mile back down to the train station, all in about an hour. We made our way across town, and I grabbed my bag. I had one way out and I wasn't sure if I was going to make it. I was beginning to doubt Einar. The train station (tog stashune) was a ways away. We covered the mile or two on foot in less than half an hour, and when we arrived with about ten minutes to spare, and Einar gave me an "I told ya so!" with a little wink. The passangers waiting to board appeared to be the business crowd. Maybe 60 or 70 people. With a few minutes to spare before the rail departed, I tried paying for a ticket. Everything was sold out. I was overcome with fear. I didn't lose my eggs but I was burning my brain trying to figure how to solve this problem. How would I catch my flight to Oslo? It looked like I would be heading to Trondheim Airport waiting for the next flight to the capital. Einar said *calm down.* Note:

Always buy transportation passes in advance. Einar calmed me down, and I followed him out onto the platform. The conductor stood at one of the entrances, and my buddy began talking to him in Norsk. A lot of words were exchanged. I didn't understand them. I squeezed in a few words in Swedish. "Jag behover tag till Oslo (I need the train to Oslo)" There was concern on my face, and I think I knew just enough of their way to connect, and verify that I was a good dude speaking their language and all. I went on listening to Einar, then Einar turned to me and said that they would let me on board. I would just have to sit in the café car, and they would let me know if a seat opened up in coach. I was ecstatic!

With my little bag on my big bag, I paid for my ticket (about $110), and walked on board. Einar followed me on. He gave me a few logistics about the train ride, then our final words became sentimental. I told him how much I appreciated his time and hospitality, and he told me how much he enjoyed having me as a guest. It was sincere. About as sincere as a pretty good moment gets. We said a good-bye, shook hands, then he get off the train. I think that's when it really hit me that I was on my way home.

It was 11:20 at night. Night is a strange term to describe time in Norway in the summer. At the time a responsible person with a day-job usually retires the day, it is still light out. Night is a deceiving and treacherous word. It describes more of a state of mind than the amount of light in the sky. It refers to that part of the day when you unwind. Some may congregate with friends. Some may enjoy the peace of a quiet drink by one's self, or a long walk through town or along the fjord. It is that part of the day when a person pays reparations to mental, and emotional well-being as they detach themselves from responsibilities of work. Night was setting in when I boarded the train. I was not sleepy, and the café car did not offer much for accommodating sleep. So, once the train got rolling, and customers cleared from the café, I walked up to the clerk and ordered a Dahl's. With beer in hand I walked the fifteen feet back to my café booth fitted with red vinyl seats and grey acrylic table. I considered my situation, and decided this would be a good opportunity to update my travel journal. The trip was still fresh in my head. It took a verbal once-over with Einar before I left to accurately site what I did each day I was in country, and the correct order of those activities. Instead of writing the full account, what I saw and what I felt and the significance of it all, I just made a record of locations, activities, and food and drink. It took close to an hour, and two Dahl's pounders before I had it all written in my journal.

The hour was close to 1:00 AM, and it was finally dark. I peered out the window at the steep, coniferous hillsides as we passed in the indigo night. The hills towered over the tracks, as the narrow rail-cut wound along. There was stoic mystery building in my soul as I peered out into the dark blue air. There was something there that I had not yet captured, and wouldn't while I was there. The darkness felt so strange. For almost the entire time I was there, I was blessed with daylight. Now I was in a café car trolling through the steep lowlands trying to figure out what hid in that brief night. I tried not to evaluate it. I tried to just love the intimate proximity of my visible range for all its intrinsic and aesthetic beauty. With my writing finished, I put the pen down, and made my way to the café for another Dahl's. As I stood in line, there was a man behind me waiting to order a Dahl's for himself. He caught my eye as I sat writing, and he returned my glance with gazes of his own. His were a little too attracted towards me. I got a little uncomfortable. I'd rather our acquaintance come to words rather than assumptions of vision and body-language. He was Euro trash by all means; the long mop on the top of his head dyed blonde, the subtle counter-culture T-shirt in '90's neon, the night train enroute for the biggest city in the country just in time for the weekend. It looked like an opportunity to have a disgusting moment in a controlled setting. How true it would be! I introduced myself as we stood in line, and the conversation flowed freely as we stood there talking. Dude came off as a little sly and a little shady, but it wasn't anything I hadn't came across at home, one time or another. And, I did not know the native language. Small handicaps. I spoke a little about myself, and he himself. He was seasonally out of work as a fisherman. He worked on the nets. His stature did not strike me as the Fisherman-type. Duties of repairing nets looked a little more his game than doing heavy lifting at sea. All in all he was nice. He made no attempts at swindling me, and spoke in English almost entirely. He asked me about my trip and I admitted disdain about not experiencing the Sami culture of Norway. He told me his heritage was Sami and Finnish. "Yi har en Dahl's" I ordered. We each got our beer and I invited him to my booth in the café car.

The trip wasn't quite yet at the halfway point, and seven hours of the Norwegian countryside from railcar isn't quite as breath-taking as one might imagine. We sat talking and laughing as I told my story about my time in Norway. When I began listening to myself talk I realized that the trip wasn't exactly exciting. It was rewarding without a doubt, but it was mostly an accumulation of subtle beauty. Norway was not a mosaic of raucous attitude, and loud drunken boasting, and brawls. Enjoying Norway was a practice of cleansing the senses, the consciousness, the mind, body, and spirit, then letting the collective energy and consciousness of such a place brood in the soul, and produce a sensation that had never before been tasted.

As I realized this, I began to shift the conversation into anecdotes of drunken nights back home, tragedies, and victories. We laughed hard, taking turns putting in our two-cents. Once Dude found out I knew how to have a good time, he invited his male, bisexual lover into our booth. Now I had two companions. Before I knew it, there would be a third.

He was about 6 feet tall, pushing three hundred pounds. I would later find out he used to be an MMA fighter. The four of us sat there talking and laughing in the wee hours of the morning. We shared stories. At one point I gave them advice. "I figured out the secret to life," I said, "And it's don't fucking die! And, if you think you might ever die, have a friend in Jesus." Our booth roared with laughter. We went on loudly for a while, and then calmed. The bisexual lover, second to join us at my booth asked me about futbol. I told him I liked it, but he wasn't buying it. I speak with reservation. I rarely get excited about things, and my calmness lead the man to believe that I was lieing. "You don't like futbol," he repeated, and I tried to argue that I did. He wasn't buying it. Our argument subsided, but for some reason the man reached across the table, hit his cup of Dahl's, spilling it all over my backpack. Splet. Spaled, speeled, spilled it with the rest running over the table and floor. My effects smelled like beer, and they would for the rest of my trip. It wasn't the mellow smell you perceived as you hold a glass of brew under your nose. No, this this was rank, and pungent. It hit the nostrils with force, causing the spine to recoil in disgust. It delivered images of a drunkard in the gutter. I could only wonder about the thoughts of others as I would pass them with my bag on the journey home.

After the beer was spilt, one of the conductors told the two bisexual men that they were getting thrown off at the next stop. The men curled up on café booths, and quickly went to sleep, avoiding their dispatching. I took up company with the MMA fighter sometime thereafter. He would occasionally shout 'Gay Pride' at the Eurotrash in the time before they went into dreamland. There I sat, in the booth of a café car enroute to Oslo at 3:15 in the morning talking about wrestling and fighting with a complete stranger. He talked with respect when I told him I wrestled for 8 years, and spent a short time training in boxing and muay thai. Unlike me this man had multiple ametuer bouts, not just a single boxing match in the campground of a river festival. I only talked about what I knew best, wrestling. That was an area of fight that, like most fighters, remained a mystery to my knew found friend. Going out on a limb, I asked him what he thought of the Russian-armbar. It was a move I didn't use often in wrestling but admired its utility in a street fight. My friend said it wasn't useful. "Not useful!" I exclaimed. "When executed correctly, it's the most effective hold a man can apply from the standing position." He agreed, but only on the grounds that any move is a good move when applied correctly. It was a point I couldn't dispute.

The technical aspects of fighting amused me, but the true thrill laid in battle. Feeling the struggle and the scope of your capabilities as you impose your will on your opponent delivered a "high" unlike anything else. In that moment, victory or defeat is felt in its most fundamental form. He told me about a fight he remembers well. It was close, and his face was bloody after two rounds. At the end of the second round he began throwing his arms in the air and looking at the crowd. The arena erupted with cheers. The energy felt between the fight and the crowd sent him onto cloud nine. He lost the match, but it was possibly the highest he ever felt. As he told me the story, I recalled matches where the whole gymnasium was roaring, and those memories connected me to the story he told. It reintroduced that amazing feeling of moral support as you exhaust every ounce of energy imposing your will on your opponent. In the end, you are tired. You are gassed. It is all you can do to just walk of the mat, but you feel accomplished (more so when you win).

The conversation led to our current state of affairs about fighting and the world. I told him I became to violent outside of training, and decided it was best that I quit. Fighting is something that rolls through your veins like a river rushing down a mountain. It becomes habitual, and you fiend for the battle. My friends said that he avoids fighting at all costs. He knows how to fight, and knows he is effective. He has nothing to prove to anyone. He has already proven everything he needs to to himself. I admitted that after my boxing match at Gauley Fest, I eventually became much more mentally stable and shared his disposition. Unlike me, he was forced out of the game instead of retiring. He had an injury that sidelined him for over a year, a broken leg. Without the rush of training and fighting, he fell into depression, and because of the depression he did nothing but eat as he waited out the healing. He went from about 200 pounds to roughly 325. The leg was now healed, and he was losing weight. He was down to about 280, still a very big man. I imagined my friend in lean condition, carrying himself at his fighting weight.

With food in mind, I told him about sharing a meal of moose-meat with my friend before leaving Trondheim. This and that was said, and I expressed my desire to go archery hunting for moose, how it would be a dream come true. The big man across from me reiterated statement Einar told me. Archery hunting was illegal in Norway. I argued on the side of archery hunters. It's a pastime that brings you closer to your prey. It's a more intimate communion with nature than hunting with a gun. My counterpart agreed with me, but he told me the government's argument, and that is that there is more of a chance of maming the animal without ever killing it. "Bullshit!" I argued. "Any good archer can shoot accurately from a distance of up to at least 30 yards. Hell," I said, "my brother can split arrows at that distance with his bow." My new friend was shocked, although I'd admit the skin is tougher and the meat much thicker on a moose than a whitetail deer. He never doubted my honesty, or at least not that I could tell. Furthermore, he was surprised. He told me that he thought that was something of myth, but I reassured him that that was just the mark of a good archer.

The conversation shifted gears, and we began talking about music as the smell of a beer-stained backpack emanated into my nostrils. Darkness was fading to light, and we were signing Johnny Cash, and drinking Dahl's in the café car at 4:00 in the morning. I had been up for 17 hours, and I was beginning to get sleepy as our dialogue slowed. The singing and drinking could only carry us so far. When daylight was fully upon us, I gave up on the Dahl's. The train began stopping at closer and closer intervals as the morning sun burned through the fog. Pastures and towns nestled into the countryside occupied the periphery of the railroad track. Closer. I could feel us getting closer to Oslo. Stops were made less than ten minutes apart. Then we started passing through tunnels. I was growing anxious with anticipation. Then with one last tunnel, we entered Oslo Flyg Platts. My friend said, "This is it!" I grabbed my bag, and unboarded. With feet on the platform, my friend and I parted ways. Onto the second leg of my trip home.

Day 7:

I walked up the stairs, moving from train-platform to airport in 10 minutes. I pulled my day-pack out of my bag as I stood in front of the kiosk, trying to get my boarding pass. I entered my code into the computer, and navigated through the prompts. On the final step, I placed my passport under the scanner. No go. I tried again only to receive the same result. I had a few hours until my flight left, but the line for baggage check-in was intimidatingly long. I moved to a different computer. Same outcome. Then, on the third different computer, a boarding pass was finally generated. Now, I just had to be patient, and not get anxious as I waited in line to check my bag in. The line felt like it was miles long, and nearly every passenger had some sort of issue that had to be resolved by the tenant at the front of the line. I inched closer and closer until it was my turn. Finally! I could see myself boarding my flight in my mind. There was resolve in my spirit! The tenant scribbled a gate and seat number on my boarding pass, and gave me directions, "You will need to claim your bag and re-check it at Newark." There was nothing left to do other than go through security and board my flight.

As I approached security, the line was moving fluidly, and continued to do so as I went through. Belt, wallet, watch, and snuff can went through the X-ray along with my day-pack, and now all I had to do was wait. I searched out my gate, and as I looked at my watch and imagined time, the prospect of Scandinavian Airlines' lounge seemed pretty attractive, mostly because I needed a WiFi connection to let my family know my phone battery was almost dead. In the world of travel, technology, particularly smart phones, are the strongest tools as well as the strongest restraints. With the capability of being connected with the other side of the world in an instant, that connection is practically expected of you. You may be able to pull up a map or flight times in the palm of your hand, but it ties you down to everything you are trying to get away from. It was important that I stayed in touch with my parents since they would be picking me up from Pittsburgh Airport that night, but it was a burden trying to keep them filled in on the progress of my travel home.

At every waypoint, I was obligated to update them on my progress. When I finally connected with the homefront from Oslo Airport, I told them I would be powering the phone down because my battery was almost dead. Little did I know there were phone chargers in the lounge. The lounge had every amentity a traveler could as for; WiFi, computers, plug-ins, fruit, cereal, juice, water, wine, beer, everything. I thought about downing a couple of pints of Carlsberg, and tying one on for the flight home, but instead, I ate some oatmeal with raisins and honey and nodded off for a half-hour nap close to my 24th hour awake. I could feel my mood shift. I was getting disinterested in my surroundings. Luckily, I wasn't in a demanding situation, but that is still the point. You need to rest and regroup when your senses get dull. I sat in a big comfortable chair, and curled up as much of my 6'2" frame as I could. When I awoke I felt a little better, I was still interested in one thing, getting home. I knew the flight would be long and uncomfortable. The layover in Newark was sure to be a nuisance. And, I had lost all interest in reading the literature I had brought along. Emerson was in my bag, "Nature, and Other Essays." I made it the whole way through nature on my way from the U.S. to Norway. I was on to the "Other Essays" on my way home, and my groggy mind and heavy eyelids wanted nothing to do with the printed word.

About 40 minutes after waking from my nap, I made my way towards my flight gate. The line at passport control was long, but moved quickly. I had my passport in hand, avoiding any delay in the system. I didn't want to be 'that guy' who held up the line.

Shuffling along, I made it through passport control, and when I arrived at my gate, my flight was already boarding. I proceeded with the flow of passengers, flashing my boarding pass, and before I knew it I was in my seat on the plane. The whole way from the moment I woke from my nap in the lounge until I was on board my flight cruised with fluidity. There were no hiccups. There were no delays. Anxiety never had a moment to set in as everything went as planned with unexpected quickness. The flight to Oslo had the long layover in New Jersey. The flight to Trondheim had been canceled, resulting in waiting in the airport all day. The long line at baggage check-in was giving me reason to believe the journey home would have the stalling time that the journey to Trondheim would have. Instead, the way home moved like a well-oiled machine. There were not the long periods of anticipation that allowed for paranoia to set in. I never had a moment to think up the 'what-if's'.

I sat in my seat, and waited for the rest of the passengers to board. That was about the closest thing to a delay in my journey that I came across. Passengers filed in, and a woman in her late 30's sat down in the seat next to me. She wore a smile, and I heard her speak a few words in English. "She's American!" I thought. I introduced myself, and we began talking about our times in Norway. Then the conversation moved on to the lives we lived back home. Another smiling face. The people I met along the road were some of the most content people I have ever met, or at least in that moment they were the most content people I have ever met. The glowing spirit of the exotic offers a newness to life that brings joy akin to that of an infant. We are once again amazed at the world around us. The exotic language and demeanor leave us riddled in their dialect. Explanation of self and environment is shed with words different from that we have grown used to, and grown callous to. Time in familiar places leaves us blind to the subtle joys of life. New aspect and perspective stimulates our soft spots. Fresh climate pokes, and prods, and makes us feel alive. The colors, textures, and structures of foreign locations distorts what we consider common, and allows the mind to construct a new skeleton of reality. The road liberates the mind, body, and soul. Sometimes you are on a quest with a destination in mind, whether that is physical, or psychological. Sometimes what you are looking for is unknown when you set out, and you just hope to find *something*. Sometimes you are trying to leave something behind. But, in each of these scenarios, a world is found that leaves you in awe. Those I have met were traveling along in a state of mild euphoria, as either you bask in what you have found, or become drunk in the possibilities of what may lay ahead.

I eased into my flight-chair. In an hour or two I fell asleep, but not for long. My slumber lasted between 60 and 90 minutes. I awoke, looked at my watch, and we weren't expected to arrive in New Jersey for another five hours. I listened to music and pod-casts for a few hours, then as the audio repeated itself a time or two, I closed the monitor, and pulled out the ear buds. The brutal reality that I was about to begin counting minutes became real. The amazing part was that once I began, time passed with consistency. It did not speed along, but I never reached a point where the seconds dragged, one after the other, inscesently anticipating the next moment to arrive and pass. I was recording, not planning. I knew the atmosphere would not change. The inside of the plane would be the inside of the plane whether we were 4 hours in, or 7 ½.

After a little more than 8 hours, we began our descent into Newark Airport. It was around 1:00 PM Eastern Standard Time when we landed. I exited the plane with my day-pack, and coursed the long maze down to baggage claim. All of us waited for a few minutes, then a terribly loud and rancid siren went off, signaling that the baggage carousel was about to begin rotating. Once again the question crossed my mind, "will my bag appear?" The tale of lost baggage left me slightly concerned at every leg of the trip where my backpack would be traveling unstrapped from my shoulders. The train was convenient; the bag would be sitting next to me. Well, mostly convenient. That little part where a pint of Dahl's got spilt onto my shit was rather inconvenient. Whenever I grabbed my bag from the carousel at Newark, the thing still smelled like beer. What would customs say? They had to have been able to smell it! I had the aroma of a drunkard, a walking brewery. Well, not much anyone could do at this point other than make judgement. That didn't bother me. If I would get stopped by authorities for how I smell, I had no contraband, so I wasn't worried.

With my stinky bag on my back, I made my way through terminal C of Newark Airport in search of gate ninety-something. I was impressed by the terminal. It was an incredible, capitalist construct. Stores, dining, everything was at my fingertips. At first glance you would not make the inference that all of these people were waiting on a flight. You would think they were out for a meal, or a drink, or for a day of shopping. I bought a coffee, for the trip in search of my gate, and cruised through the crowd, hoping not to be consumed by it. Savages, every last one of them, all preying on consumer goods. My gate was at the far end of the building. I had a few hours until my flight would be boarding, so I sat down and did some reading. As my left ear was being filled with a conversation composed mostly of middle-aged, suburban bullshit on a slightly self-indulged level, I was about to leave and get a beer. There was a bar-and-grill I had passed on the way that looked like they would be able to accommodate my desires. Then an African woman sat down next to me. I can't recall if I addressed her, or her to me, but we started talking, and our words and ideas pulled me away from condescending criticism, and I enjoyed her company. Dialogue subsided, and in our silence, I felt like I should leave her to her concerns. I was ready for that beer. Back through the American Dream. I sat at the bar situated in the main hallway of Terminal C, and ordered a beer off the computer, and paid with my credit card. I could not believe how automated the consumer would had become in recent years. Before long, prostitution rings will be ran from the internet with a payment option of direct deposit. Amidst all the chaos of the airport, I was served. It was probably an IPA. I hadn't had much of that in Norway. It was there I just chose to go with something different most of the time. My thirst for blondes and stouts had been fulfilled. I was closing ground towards home, and I thought it suitable for my taste-buds to feel the same way my consciousness was beginning to feel. I sat at the bar, across from a family, most likely from North-Jersey; a husband and wife in their early fifties, and a son and girlfriend in their twenties. The father was short tempered. His income highly surpassed his intelligence as well as his patience. I was beginning to have enough of that place. I finished my beer, and headed back towards my gate.

    When I arrived at the gate, the waiting room was relatively empty. Two flights boarded in the time since I left for a beer. Amongst the few people currently waiting to board flights was a young man with a familiar haircut. It appeared as though we were waiting on the same flight. I approached him, and asked if he was heading to Pittsburgh. In a familiar accent, he said he was. Between the haircut, and the accent I was beginning to believe he was Norwegian. "Maybe I'm just jaded for the past week," I thought. I asked him where he was from. His answer assured my assumption. The man was Norwegian with a tall, thin frame, a dirty blonde mop of hair, long on top with short sides, that airy, flowing accent, and a can of snus. I told him that I suspected him to be Norwegian, and he was a little bashful about the comment. I wasn't condescending, but I figured I would let the matter die. As we sat waiting for our flight, I felt a strange familiarity with the young man. It was as though we had spent much time together, and found comfort in each other's presence. His accent, appearance, and mannerism took me back. Once again I was in Trondheim with a friend. A polite and energetic buddy was with me as we waited in the airport. His name was Henrik. He told me he was on his way to meet his girlfriend who lived in Pittsburgh. I was surprised at him making the journey by himself at the age of 18. He brushed it off telling me he had been traveling along since 13. Both of his parents worked in the airline industry, and he was very familiar with airports, and international travel.

Before long our gate got changed. We trotted across the terminal together. Then it got changed again, and again. The two of us spent nearly an hour chasing our flight gate together. As we did, I felt a universal connection with the Norwegian culture. He never left me for dead when my shoes came untied, and I waited for him as well. It was as though Henrik and I were already friends from the moment words were spoken. There was a friendliness about him that spoke to the tones and rhythms of the land in which I had been inhabiting for the past week, a warm hospitality of the here-and-now, and of things intangible. There was no reason for reserve or discomfort. There was no reason to be guarded. We had the same goal, catch the flight, and having a partner in the effort freed the mind from any stress. The pouch of snus he offered me was an extension of the connection I felt with him. The tobacco was strong. I hadn't had a pinch in a few hours, and as I swallowed the juices, my esophagus began to burn. Henrik got a little kick out of my reaction. He warned me it was strong stuff, and it definitely hit the mark.

Before I got strong heartburn, or sick, I took the pouch out and tossed it in the trash. Our flight finally boarded. We sat at opposite ends of the plane in the hour-long flight from Newark to Pittsburgh. When we deplaned, we continued along together to baggage claim. I met my parents, and he his girlfriend. We waved at each other from across the room as we left. Two hours later I was at home asleep. Over the past 41 hours I got roughly 90 minutes of sleep.

The trip was a trip. I couldn't have asked for more. Especially, considering the fact that traveling really takes it out of you. Whatever that "it" is. Mostly energy, but a little bit of whatever ego and emotion you've had built up over time as well. If the soul is unrest, then go somewhere where you feel you should go. But most importantly, manage your money well, and go! 'Till next time, peace my friends!

Made in the USA
Monee, IL
25 September 2022